OXFORD CLASSICAL & PHILOSOPHICAL MONOGRAPHS

NOTE

The works published in this series are concerned with subjects falling within the scope of the Faculty of Literae Humaniores, viz. Greek and Latin Language and Literature, Ancient History, and Philosophy

Philosophical

CONSENT, FREEDOM AND POLITICAL OBLIGATION, by J. P. Plamenatz (*Out of print*)

MORALITY AND FREEDOM IN THE PHILOSOPHY OF IMMANUEL KANT, by W. T. Jones (*Out of print*)

AN EXAMINATION OF THE DEDUCTIVE LOGIC OF JOHN STUART MILL, by Reginald Jackson (*Out of print*)

REASON AND CONDUCT IN HUME'S TREATISE, by Rachael M. Kydd (*Out of print*)

THE MORAL SENSE, by D. Daiches Raphael (*Out of print*)

KNOWLEDGE AND THE GOOD IN PLATO'S REPUBLIC, by H. W. B. Joseph (*Out of print*)

JOHN LOCKE AND THE WAY OF IDEAS, by John W. Yolton

Classical (including History)

THE STOICHEDON STYLE IN GREEK INSCRIPTIONS, by R. P. Austin (*Out of print*)

COINAGE OF DAMASTION, by J. M. F. May

AINOS: ITS HISTORY AND COINAGE 474–341 B.C., by J. M. F. May (*Out of print*)

TRAJAN'S PARTHIAN WAR, by F. A. Lepper

GALEN ON JEWS AND CHRISTIANS, by R. Walzer

MARGINALIA SCAENICA, by John Jackson

LAWS AND EXPLANATION IN HISTORY, by William Dray

THE RHODIAN PERAEA AND ISLANDS, by P. M. Fraser and G. E. Bean

THE NATURE OF HISTORICAL EXPLANATION

BY

PATRICK GARDINER

GREENWOOD PRESS, PUBLISHERS
WESTPORT, CONNECTICUT

Library of Congress Cataloging-in-Publication Data

Gardiner, Patrick L., 1922–
   The nature of historical explanation.

   Reprint. Originally published: London ; New York :
Oxford University Press, 1952.
   Includes index.
   1. History--Philosophy. I. Title. II. Title:
Historical explanation.
D16.9.G34 1985   901   85-21911
ISBN 0-313-24976-8 (lib. bdg. : alk. paper)

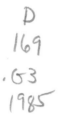
Copyright Oxford University Press 1952

This reprint has been authorized by the Oxford University Press

Reprinted in 1985 by Greenwood Press
A division of Congressional Information Service, Inc.
88 Post Road West, Westport, Connecticut 06881

Printed in the United States of America

10 9 8 7 6 5 4 3 2 1

FOREWORD

MY thanks are due in the first place to Mr. Isaiah Berlin and Mr. W. H. Walsh for the extremely valuable guidance and encouragement they gave me at various stages in the writing of this book.

I am also indebted to Sir David Ross and Professor H. J. Paton who, as members of the Classical and Philosophical Monographs Committee, read the book in proofs and typescript respectively, and provided many helpful suggestions: and, further, I am very grateful for criticism and advice I have received from various of my friends: in particular, Mr. David Pears, Mr. Richard Wollheim, and Mr. Brian McGuinness. Finally, I wish to acknowledge a general and considerable debt to the writings and lectures of Professor Gilbert Ryle for my approach to a number of the problems treated.

P. G.

OXFORD
March 1952

CONTENTS

INTRODUCTION

THE expression 'the philosophy of history' has come to have various associations. By some it may be regarded as signifying a submarine monster, dredged from the deep waters of nineteenth-century metaphysics, its jaws occasionally opening to emit prophecies in a dead (or at any rate a foreign) tongue—the language of Hegelian dialectic. By some it is thought to be a mysterious subject, not quite philosophy, and yet again, not quite history, but a kind of vaguely disreputable amalgam of both. Alternatively, it may be held that books on the philosophy of history are in a sense manuals for doing history, rather as a manual on fly-fishing might, at a stretch, be termed 'the theory of fly-fishing'. And the latter supposition is encouraged by the ambiguity of the word 'history'; for when we use the word we may, on the one hand, be taken to be referring to the past events, activities, thoughts, and so forth about which historians write—when, for example, we say that Jones's researches are leading to the discovery of much of the history of the last few years, or when we remark that history repeats itself: on the other hand, we may be taken as referring to the books, pamphlets, or lectures historians produce to describe what has happened—when we state, for instance, that Smith is reading history. And a concentration upon the first of the above senses of the word may lead to the belief that the type of investigation pursued by the philosopher of history is of the same order as the type of investigation pursued by the historian, the difference being that the philosopher occupies a privileged position or vantage-point from which he is enabled to survey the entire historical process, not only pointing out characteristics of past events unnoticed by the practising historian, but in addition telling us what the future will be like before it actually occurs. The philosopher is expected to answer questions about the meaning or purpose of the historical process, the nature of human destiny, the course of human history, and the future of mankind.

There is, however, another procedure open to a philosopher who is nervous of appropriating to himself the status of a prophet or a seer. Such a philosopher may withhold the claim to write (or rewrite) history altogether, without admitting thereby that he has lost his occupation. For, he may legitimately argue, it is possible that the function of the philosopher has been misconstrued, or, at any rate, that it has been unduly restricted.

Philosophy may be said to concern itself with various branches of knowledge, but it does not therefore follow that it is itself such a branch of knowledge. The philosopher may discuss scientific method or ethics or the assumptions of common-sense, but he is not for that reason a scientist or a moralist or even a 'plain man'. Someone may, without being impossibly paradoxical, assert that history or psychology is really common-sense; but were someone to remark that philosophy is really common-sense, it would be difficult to know what reply to make.

And so the philosopher, it may be contended, can indeed consider history, but this does not imply that he must ask concerning it the same kind of questions that the historian asks. We may distinguish between questions asked *within* history and questions asked *about* it. Historians answer the first sort of question, philosophers answer the second sort. Thus an historian may try to answer the question: 'Was there a connexion between the Protestant Reformation of the sixteenth and seventeenth centuries, and the emergence of a capitalist economy?' A philosopher, on the other hand, would not be interested in the truth or falsehood of the answer given by the historian to this question, but he would be very interested in the kind of evidence an historian might bring forward to substantiate his claim, in the criteria he uses for deciding whether or not a connexion existed.

It is apparent that there is a large number of questions that both can be, and are, asked *about* history. There are questions like: 'Is history a science?', 'How can we know historical facts?', 'Is there any such thing as an objective historical account?', 'What is the nature of historical "theories" and interpretations—the Marxian, for example?', 'Are there historical laws?'. These are questions which genuinely give rise to puzzlement and it is difficult to see who, other than the philosopher, is in a position to attempt their answer. Thus, however sceptical we may be about the philosopher's qualifications elsewhere, it would appear that here at least there is work for him to do.

But what form should this work take? There is a temptation, when treating of any branch of knowledge, to ask the big questions first, and, having answered them, to deal with the subject along a course set by those answers. And, while this method may have its value, it is also open to considerable disadvantages. For example, the question 'Is history a science?' is a question dangerous in its simplicity, particularly so because to call some branch of study 'scientific' is frequently a means of giving it an air, if not of glamour, then at any rate of respectability. And all too often bold attempts to give a straight 'yes' or 'no' answer to the question, supported by reasons, end up in verbal disputes amounting to little more than alternative linguistic recommendations. This in turn results in a form of intellectual claustrophobia: the objections as they swarm in have to be met by a continual adjustment or alteration of the normal usage of certain expressions.

Perhaps unsatisfactory consequences like these are attributable to a too naïve approach, a tendency to view such questions as: 'Is history a science?' as like the question: 'Is a whale a mammal?' which can be settled by appealing to certain accepted criteria. We demand a simple cut-and-dried answer, and then are dissatisfied when it is given.

The question: 'What is the nature of historical explanation?' is, I suggest, dangerous in that way. For it implies that, provided a careful enough search is conducted, a 'clear and distinct idea' of what historical explanation really *is* may somewhere be found, and, with labour, brought to light. And yet, when philosophers have claimed to have brought it to light their discoveries have been as unsatisfying as they have been various. And there is a further disadvantage. The philosopher who claims to have discovered the essence, simple and distilled, of historical explanation is in danger of laying himself open to the embarrassing accusation that he is trying to teach the historian the rules of his profession, that he is prescribing to the historian how he ought to write history.

In what follows an attempt will be made to approach the topic by a different route. I shall, it is true, start by giving an outline of the 'regularity' interpretation of explanation, but this outline will only be regarded as being in the nature of a 'marker' or sketch-map according to which bearings can be taken. How far it is possible to regard all historical explanations, or even some, as approximating to this pattern, how far the objections philosophers have marshalled against such an assimilation are justified, how far the alternative interpretations suggested correspond to the historian's actual procedure in certain cases; these represent the kind of questions that will have to be considered. On such a programme, perhaps little of a spectacular nature can be expected in the way of results; but for a subject where the temptation to provide clear-cut and over-simplified solutions is rarely absent this may not be a wholly undesirable feature. And by trying to keep the actual practice of historians constantly in view we may at least be able to see some of the disputes that have raged concerning the 'philosophy of history' in a truer perspective.

PART I
EXPLANATION IN SCIENCE AND EVERYDAY LIFE

§ 1. *The Logic of Explanation*

'EXPLANATION' is a vague concept. We may explain somebody's headache by saying that he has been sitting too long in the sun or that he has been working too hard, but we may also explain it by saying that it is a symptom of an oncoming attack of influenza. We may explain somebody's manners by saying that he has been badly brought up, but we may also explain them by saying that he has an unfortunate personality. We may explain somebody's arithmetical calculation by saying that he learnt mathematics at school, but we may also explain it by saying that he has observed the rules of long division.

Hume, and empiricists generally, have been wont to assume that all explanation takes the form of relating one event, the *explicandum*, to another event or set of events which 'cause' or 'condition' it. This, as will be shown in detail later, is not true: nevertheless, since it represents an important form of explanation as it occurs both in common life and in the sciences, I shall begin by considering it, first presenting it in its 'bare bones', and then treating it in the various contexts of its occurrence.

Hume argued that when we are said to explain an event, we refer to another event, or set of events, of a type which has always been observed in our previous experience to accompany the type of event to be explained. Another way of putting this is to say that an event is explained when it is brought under a generalization or law. It becomes an instance of a general rule stating that, given the presence of certain initial conditions, events similar to the one to be explained will occur. Such a rule or universal hypothesis may be regarded as asserting a regularity of the following type: whenever an event of a specified kind C occurs at a certain place and time, an event of a specified kind E will occur at a place and time which is related in a specified manner to the place and time of the first event. Thus the explanation of a given event consists in (1) stating a universal law, or set of laws, (2) stating the existence of a set of initial conditions $C_1 . . . . C_n$, so that from these two statements a third statement describing the event in question follows.[1]

I assume that, as an outline of the general pattern taken by explanation in science, and also of the general pattern taken by many explanations on the level of common sense, this account is substantially correct. Thus, in answer to the stock question: 'Why did the billiard-ball move?' it may be said that another billiard-ball came into collision with it; and it may be added, perhaps, that the surface of the billiard-table was normal (i.e. it was of even texture, not adhesive, &c.) and that the billiard-balls were 'real' billiard-balls (e.g. not disguised bombs which explode when struck). These represent the initial conditions of the billiard-ball's movement and explain its occurrence. But they only do so in virtue of a generalization, not necessarily stated, to the effect that whenever conditions of the kind mentioned are fulfilled the billiard-ball will move. It is this general rule, established by observation of the behaviour of billiard-balls on past occasions, that warrants our giving the explanation that we do give when, on a particular occasion, a billiard-ball is observed to move after it has been struck by another. For, were this not so, we should only be able to say: 'Billiard-ball A struck billiard-ball B, and billiard-ball B moved'; the force of the word 'because' derives from the fact that a particular case has been seen to satisfy the requirements of a causal law, and it is to this causal law that we must appeal if our explanation is questioned.

The 'logical structure' of explanations of this kind is the same as that of predictions. A predictive statement about a future event is derived from a statement concerning a num-

---

[1] See K. R. Popper, *Logik der Forschung*, and quotations from this work in the same author's *The Open Society and Its Enemies*, vol. ii, pp. 248, 249.

ber of known conditions taken in conjunction with another statement asserting a general law. Thus an astronomer may forecast the positions of the planets at a future date by knowing their present configuration and by knowing certain laws of celestial mechanics. And so, while in explanation the emphasis is centred upon determining the conditions of the event that confronts us, in prediction it is centred upon the effect that a set of given conditions produces. (It is perhaps worth noting in this context that the notions of past and future, which in ordinary life are regarded as the features principally distinguishing an explanation from a prediction, do not enter into functional explanation, as it occurs in the advanced sciences, at all; for there considerations of time-order are superseded by considerations relating solely to structural order.)

The same pattern is again evident when generalizations or laws are tested. Both in common experience and in science we are interested in the formulation of rules concerning the way things behave, yet this interest takes different forms. While the engineer, for instance, necessarily takes into account the laws of mechanics when building a particular bridge, we find scientists interested in the reliability or otherwise of the laws in themselves, the laws which engineers (or architects or doctors) are content to take for granted as the means towards achieving whatever end they may have in view. To find out if a law holds, and can be relied upon, it must be tested or confirmed. Confirmation follows the structure of explanation and prediction. An event is said to confirm a law when its occurrence verifies a statement that follows as a consequence from other statements asserting the law in question and the presence of the requisite conditions for its application; and a law may be said to be falsified when the verificatory event does not occur. Thus the behaviour of the planet Uranus together with the assumption of certain physical laws led to the postulation of the existence of another planet; the existence of this planet was subsequently verified by the observation of the planet Neptune; and this latter observation may, according

to our point of view, be regarded (1) as providing an explanation of the behaviour of the planet Uranus, (2) as verifying a
prediction, and (3) as confirming the physical laws in question.[1]

It would be a mistake, however, to suppose that explanation
is concerned only with the correlation of events. It is true
that when the explanation of a particular phenomenon is asked
for, it is given in terms of a correlation between the phenomenon referred to and other phenomena that have been
observed regularly to accompany it on past occasions. Suppose, however, that we now demand a further explanation;
suppose that, having been informed that the planets obey
Kepler's laws, i.e. that they move in ellipses round the sun,
that they describe equal areas in equal time, and that the
centres of their mean distances vary as the squares of their
periodic times, we then ask: 'Yes, but *why* do they do this?'
The answer will be that they are bodies and hence obey
Newton's laws.

Newton's laws represent laws of a higher level of generality;
that is to say, they are concerned, not merely with the planets,
but with all bodies of whatever kind. Given the fact that the
planets are bodies of a certain description, and given the laws
of Newtonian physics, we are in a position to deduce Kepler's
laws of planetary motion. But, it may be asked, how does that
explain Kepler's laws? In this sense: with the help of Newton's
laws and certain empirical data concerning various types of
bodies we can deduce laws governing a very wide range of
phenomena; what has happened, in fact, is that Newton's
laws make possible an extensive correlation between the movements of the planets and a large number of other phenomena.
A higher generalization has been produced that serves to
explain, as sub-laws within a system, other generalizations
which previously had been considered to be separate and
distinct. The progress of science has been a constant movement in the direction of subsuming known laws under laws
of higher generality and of a consequently wider application.

Thus explanation, both in science and in common life,

---

[1] See K. R. Popper, op. cit.

implies the formulation of laws or generalizations. This would appear to eliminate the possibility that we are doing something radically different in kind when we speak on the level of common sense from what we are doing when we speak on the level of science. We explain our headaches, our insomnia, our good health, and so forth by correlating them with other happenings like sitting too long in the sun, drinking strong black coffee, and taking regular exercise, which have been observed to accompany the events and states to be explained both in our own experience and in the experience of others. We explain the movements of the planets by referring to certain correlations observed to hold between bodies of different sizes and in various positions. The procedure appears to be fundamentally the same in both types of cases. We have, however, noticed that there are significant differences between the generality and scope of some laws and those of others, and we have touched upon the important relations which may subsist between them. And this brings us to a point where the methods of science and common sense must be compared and examined more closely.

§ 2. *Scientific and Commonsense Explanation*

THE primary difficulty of discussing the affinities and the differences between scientific and commonsense forms of explanation lies in the extreme vagueness of the terms 'science' and 'common sense'. On the one hand, there is the familiar view that common sense, when 'organized', *is* science; and, on the other, there appear to be important and often fundamental differences between the various branches of inquiry that are, or may be, loosely called 'scientific' which give rise to a multitude of border-line cases and half-way houses. Is modern psychology a science, or is it just common sense dressed up in an impressive-sounding jargon? What are we to say of meteorology or, still more doubtful, of philology? And what of the so-called social sciences? Is history a science?

Some of these questions must be laid aside as outside the scope of the present work: others will have to be considered in detail later. For the present only broad distinctions can be made, only the crudest lines drawn. The *nuances* must wait.

'Common sense' may be conveniently regarded as a name for those skills used by human beings in making their way about the world. To say that a person has common sense is to say, roughly, that he can be relied upon to act in ways that are likely to enable him to achieve such ends as he sets himself with a reasonable degree of success. Practical life requires for its effective conduct a capacity to make rapid *ad hoc* decisions and judgements guided by past experiences recognized to be relevant to situations as they arise.[1] It does not always, though it may, require lengthy ratiocination, since there are occasions when—as experience again teaches us—delay is fatal. For the same reasons, it is not always necessary to have attained a high degree of certainty about the facts of a situation and the possible consequences of various courses of action before deciding to act in a certain way. I do not need to be absolutely certain that I will not kill myself before deciding to jump out of a first-floor window in order to escape the flames that are scorching my back. Nor do I have to know the precise intensity of the heat making things so uncomfortable for me in order to know that my remaining very much longer in my present situation will have unfortunate results so far as I am concerned. High degrees of precision and certainty are largely irrelevant to common sense. Again 'common sense', in its usual connotation, is not confined to any particular narrowly defined aspect of experience: it is used rather to refer to the recipes, maxims, and hand-to-mouth expedients we utilize to cope with the innumerable and varying problems that everyday life sets us to solve. When we act 'according to common sense' we fall back upon past experience but we do not concentrate our attention upon any particular feature of it. 'Common sense' is frequently used in contrast to 'expert knowledge' and to 'science'. It is as contrasted with the latter that its principal interest lies in this context.

---

[1] This is not intended to exclude the largely habitual character of much of our daily behaviour. See below, § 3.

The immense variety and complexity of the situations with which everyday life presents us are also reflected indirectly in the nature of our ordinary language. The primary uses of language from a practical point of view involve the communication of information and the expression of commands, directions, wishes, advice, and so on. Its function is to facilitate action by classifying various features of the world to secure their easy recognition and to relate them to our past experience. And, since life is an immensely complicated affair, which requires, if we are to be able to make sense of it and achieve our ends, constant simplification and at the .same time constant reorientation, our language must necessarily be selective, flexible, and adaptable.

We may dovetail the two points that have just been made by saying that ordinary language is the language of common sense. Our practical recipes for coping with the problems of everyday life are expressed in a language that is adapted to express their essential 'looseness' and lack of precision. Philosophers have often found fault with this characteristic of language, thus basically misconceiving its purpose and ignoring its usefulness. And in attempting to remedy the 'disease' they have sought to impose upon the words or concepts of ordinary usage a precision and tightness which is unsuited to their function and which has led to the emergence of insoluble puzzles.

As common sense may be contrasted with science, so ordinary language may be contrasted with the language used by scientists. The various branches of scientific inquiry represent investigations into different fields of phenomena. The scientist aims to go beyond the crude rough-and-ready generalizations that are a feature of common sense. As a specialist in the behaviour of certain types of phenomena, his researches are concentrated within the limits of his chosen subject-matter. Natural science is misleadingly called the 'science of Nature', since this is likely to give the impression that the field of inquiry of the scientist is the entire range of natural phenomena, considered *en masse*. Whereas it is a distinguishing feature of science to break up the immense bulk of the 'given', to seek to elicit from it more or less independent sub-systems within which correlations of varying degrees of precision and universality may be established. And while it is, of course, true that all science must proceed from the data of common sense, from the things of ordinary perceptual experience and from the fragmentary generalizations of commonsense inductive procedure, yet, as the observational instruments and experimental techniques of each branch of scientific inquiry evolve, so the original correlations are replaced by others of a very different kind.[1] And, reflecting these developments, new descriptive methods become necessary, adapted to the accurate expression of the new discoveries and to their systematic representation. The language of common sense proves too cumbersome and imprecise for this purpose, the advanced sciences, for example, finding in mathematics the vehicle for the formulation of their theories and hypotheses.[2]

What has been said clearly has a bearing upon the problem of the distinction between common sense and scientific explanation. For it accounts, not only for the difficulties in which so many philosophers have become entangled who have tried to reduce all cases of explanation to cases of 'cause' and 'effect', but also for the many paradoxical statements that have been made on the other side, which suggest it is really nonsense to speak in causal terms at all. Thus Russell writes (op. cit., p. 180) that 'the complete extrusion [of the word 'cause'] from the philosophical vocabulary is desirable' and 'the reason why physics has ceased to look for causes is that, in fact, there are no such things'. And, in a like manner, and for reasons that are obscure, Neurath[3] attacks the use of a causal terminology in the 'social sciences' (not precisely

---

[1] Succinctly described by Russell: 'In short, every advance in a science takes us further away from the crude uniformities which are first observed, into greater differentiation of antecedent and consequent, and into a continually wider circle of antecedents recognized as relevant' (*Mysticism and Logic*, p. 188).

[2] This point is well brought out by Stuart Hampshire in an article, 'Logical Necessity', *Philosophy*, Oct. 1948.

[3] Otto Neurath, 'Foundations of the Social Sciences', *International Encyclopaedia of Unified Science*, vol. ii, no. 1.

defined) as a 'clumsy way of speaking of the correlation of two items within an aggregation', proposing rather surprisingly that in place of 'cause' and 'effect' should be substituted such expressions as 'arising from' and 'growing out of' (the weakness of the recommended procedure suggesting that the analogy drawn between physics and sociology is, at least at the present stage of the latter's development, not as close as Neurath apparently wishes to assume).

The relation between commonsense explanation and scientific explanation will be treated in the following manner: first, the usage of 'cause' in ordinary discourse will briefly be examined; secondly, I shall consider the aims and structure of forms of explanation in the sciences; and, thirdly, I shall enter into more detail concerning the confusions that have arisen between the two.

On the classical view of causality, it was thought that the cause of an event had a certain definite duration, and that, immediately it had run its course, the effect came into operation, the process of effects following causes being envisaged as a system of shifts or sentry-go. But this conception will not bear analysis, for difficulties begin when it is asked at what point the dividing line is to be drawn between the cause and the effect. There must, according to the theory, be an instant at which the cause ceases, and another instant at which the effect starts. But if time is regarded as a series of instants, it must also be clear that there can be no contiguous instants, for between any two such instants it is always possible to interpose another, however close the two instants are imagined to be. And there is accordingly no instant immediately contiguous upon another at which the cause may be said to end and the effect to start. Problems also arise when the events termed 'cause' and 'effect' are considered. For these are both processes and so divisible into parts. It may then be asked: 'Which part is the cause?' If we answer that the cause is the part directly preceding the effect, that it is the final momentary instant before the effect begins, we are then confronted with the difficulty that it is still possible to interpose an infinite number of similar instants between any two selected, and our search for a cause corresponding to the last instant of a process resolves itself into an infinite regress of point events. And thus the use of the causal concept would be impossible.

Yet not only is it used; it also proves extremely convenient. And this returns us to considerations of the function of ordinary language that were noted above. 'Cause' and 'effect', as used in daily life, do not possess the precision the foregoing analysis in terms of fixed duration, immediate contiguity, and so forth attempts to give them. The practical questions of normal life do not require for their solution an array of 'stiff' concepts with clearly defined edges; the opposite is the case. In order to light a match it is sufficient to know that striking it will achieve the desired effect. It is not necessary to ask whether the cause really begins with taking the match out of the box; or with the contact of the match-head against the sand-paper; or with the spark that precedes the actual ignition of the match. Anybody who began to raise questions of this type when presented with a box of matches would not be taken seriously, for they are not questions that can be legitimately asked about terms whose elasticity is essential to their meaning and utility.

Our analysis of the causal concept must be appropriate to the level of language upon which we are speaking. The idea of causality is a function of a given language, requiring adjustment according to the particular level of language upon which it is used.[1] On certain levels, as will be seen, the nature of the correlations involved makes the use of causality practically impossible. But not all empirical inquiries have attained to the structure of physics, and not all terminologies exclude the possibility of speaking causally. To say, with Russell, that 'there are no such things' as causes, is to recommend that all language should be assimilated to the language of the physicist.

What is to be called the 'cause' of an event in a given instance is a question to be decided in terms of the field of

[1] I owe this point to a lecture by Dr. F. Waismann.

inquiry involved, and of the interests and purposes of the speaker. When common sense says that an attack of pneumonia was caused by standing too long in the cold, and medical science says that it was caused by such factors as the presence of pneumococci and the physical condition of the patient as indicated by his past clinical history, it is not proper to say that the commonsense assessment of the causes is right and the scientific wrong, or vice versa. There is no conflict; the word 'cause' is merely being used differently in the two cases.

For common sense, the cause of an event is frequently conceived of as being a kind of handle, an instrument for achieving, or helping to achieve, an end that we desire. We say that striking a match causes it to light: but, of course, this is not the *only* condition of the match's catching fire. The match must not be damp or a dummy, the sand-paper must not be worn out, the match must be struck with a certain minimum degree of force, and so forth. I could, if I chose, make a list of all these conditions, but it is not usually worth my while to do so. There is a sense, even, where it would be true to say that the factory of Messrs. Bryant & May is the cause of this match's lighting, but on most occasions there would be little point in stating this truth. If I want a fire, I want to know how to produce the flame that will set the faggots alight; and I am not interested in all the additional conditions that make this possible, apart from the striking of the match. (Naturally, if I were a match manufacturer, I might very well be interested in them.) Common sense is selective; and it selects as the causes of events those features that can be utilized for their production (or, alternatively, prevention). And so, when a causal statement of this type is made, it is not supposed that it will *always* hold in all possible circumstances, or that the cause mentioned is the 'true' or the 'real' cause in the sense of excluding the relevance of any other conditions. This is shown by the fact that exceptions to a causal statement like 'striking the match causes it to light' are accounted for by saying, not that the statement is false, but that it is only true, 'other things being equal', and that in this instance the 'other things'—the state of the sand-paper, the pressure exerted by the fingers on the match—were not up to the mark. And this is a tacit admission that the condition chosen as the 'cause' was only one among many conditions that were also relevant. What we choose to regard as the cause of an event is largely dependent upon its practical value. When the causes of war are being investigated, for instance, it may be decided that both economic factors and human psychology are relevant to its outbreak; yet since we deem it to be within our power to influence or alter the economic system of a society, whereas the control of human psychology seems, at least at present, to be beyond our capacity, we are likely to regard the economic rather than the psychological factors as the 'cause' of war. Another, simpler, example of the conditions governing the selection of causes occurred quite recently at an inquiry into a railway accident. A soldier, wishing to get home quickly, had pulled the communication cord; the train had stopped; and shortly afterwards another train had collided with it. It was emphasized at the inquiry that the pulling of the communication cord was not the cause of the accident, since, if certain other regulations relating to this contingency had been adhered to, the accident would not have taken place. Yet, on the other hand, it was clear enough that, had the communication cord not been pulled, the accident again would not have taken place. The choice of which of the conditions was to be regarded as the 'cause' of the event was thus made upon practical considerations.

The differences between the techniques and terminologies of the various branches of empirical science are sufficiently great to make a comparison between the modes of explanation they employ and the modes employed by common sense extremely difficult within a survey as short as this must necessarily be. The dangers of over-simplification are very great. It is advisable to begin by considering a relatively undeveloped science where the gap separating it from common sense would not seem to be so large as is the case with certain other branches of inquiry. The example I propose to take is the example of Freudian psychology.[1]

The concepts of psycho-analysis must be sharply differentiated from those that occur in the more advanced sciences in that they function in a system which does not (at present) employ standards of measurement to any significant degree. Yet there is a sense in which psycho-analytical method may legitimately be termed 'scientific'. Psycho-analysts confine themselves to the detailed explanation of 'phenomena within fairly clearly specified limits: they are concerned to explain such specific phenomena as, for instance, slips of the tongue and pen, dreams, 'unintended' actions, and, more generally, the patterns of human behaviour and motivation and the manifestations of psychological disturbance. This has been done in terms of the experiences undergone by the individual human being at various times during his life. The psycho-analyst also claims to be able to control (within limits and in certain types of cases) the nature and direction of future individual behaviour: the therapeutic feature of psycho-analytical procedure has always been a predominant characteristic of the method as a whole. To achieve these results, psycho-analysts have found it convenient to introduce large-scale unifying hypotheses, like the theory of unconscious mental activity, which have proved fruitful in explaining

---

[1] It should be added, nevertheless, that this example has only a limited relevance in the present context. There are features of it which sharply distinguish it both from the methodology of other branches of science and from the form of commonsense causal explanation so far considered. It has been pointed out, for, instance, that psycho-analysts speak in terms of *motives* and *intentions* rather than of *causes* and *generalizations* (see 'The Logical Status of Psycho-Analysis', by Stephen Toulmin, *Analysis*, Dec. 1948), and much philosophical work remains to be done if the muddles that have gathered round Freudian techniques are to be resolved. Freud's own emphasis on the unconscious as 'something actual and tangible' (*Introductory Lectures on Psycho-Analysis*', p. 235) and on the causation of acts by 'mental processes' (op. cit., p. 234) does not help matters. All the same, there are, I think, good grounds for treating of it here, (1) because it is at any rate *partially* concerned with establishing correlations—correlations, for example, between certain types of infantile experience and adolescent and adult behaviour, and (2) because it exemplifies clearly the growth of a conceptual system adapted to its discoveries. And these two features of the study would seem to justify our assimilating its procedure to that of the other sciences, however much it may differ in other respects.

many apparently unrelated and unaccountable aspects of human behaviour, in a manner which at any rate bears analogies to the success of certain hypotheses in, say, physics or chemistry, the success, to take an instance, of the hypotheses of molecular motion in explaining Boyle's law, Charles's law, and other laws of gases.

Thus psycho-analysis forms, to some extent, an organized system. That is to say, it is more than a mere collection of separate, or only loosely related, statements made about people's behaviour. Many of the *Maximes* of la Roche-foucauld, or Chesterfield's letters, contain generalizations about such behaviour—very acute ones. But although, in a loose manner of speaking, we might truly say that la Roche-foucauld was a good psychologist much as people say that Shakespeare was a good one, no one would consider that he was doing, or attempting to do, the kind of thing Freud and his followers have been doing. And this is due, not only to the fact that Freud developed a large-scale and effective thera-peutic technique, or to the fact that he was interested primarily in the behaviour of neurotic individuals where the writers of maxims have confined their attention to the behaviour of normal people. For it is clear that neither of these features is fundamental to the Freudian system, although both may be said to follow from it. As an applied scientist, like the engineer, is able to make use of mechanical laws to design a bridge capable of withstanding a certain load, so, in a roughly analogous way, the psycho-analyst is able to make use of the laws he formulates about psychological phenomena to effect cures in particular cases; nor, obviously, are his laws confined to the behaviour of abnormal persons, for, were this the case, it would be impossible to explain the divergence of behaviour from the normal which these persons manifest, and hence to attempt therapy at all. The fundamental point is rather that Freudian psychology has not merely taken note of the generalizations that acute 'observers of human nature' have made, has not merely tabulated or listed cases of, say, people not acting from the motives they consciously believe themselves to be acting from, but has tried to bring generalizations of this type under wider theories, like the theories of the Unconscious or of infantile sexuality, by means of which, it is held, such established generalizations can be explained, and fresh ones derived or suggested. The precise status of these theories is at present uncertain, and the uncertainty is not lessened by disagreements within the profession itself regarding their validity and correct interpretation: such disagreements characterize a science as yet in an early stage. For it is a distinguishing mark of an advanced science that there should exist accepted criteria for the confirmation and falsification of theories, and well-defined public methods for the verification of results; and it is to the lack of both of these in much psycho-analytical work that the disagreements mentioned above bear witness. Nevertheless, this does not alter the element of organization, of system, in psycho-analysis, which is a necessary, although not a sufficient, condition of a branch of inquiry's being termed 'scientific'.

The systematic character of a science is important for our inquiry in the following way. We commonly say that the psychologist (or physicist or biologist) 'knows what to look for', knows what features of the case before him require his attention, when he is giving an explanation of a specific event; in other words, he knows what is relevant or irrelevant to his investigation. Just as a physicist will not take account of the colour of an object when considering the speed with which it falls to the ground, so the psychologist will not take account of the month of a person's birth when he is trying to diagnose his conviction that he is being persecuted by pink rabbits. He may, on the other hand, be interested in the patient's childhood experiences, for these he may consider to be relevant. What is it that makes possible such judgements of relevance and irrelevance? This is an extremely important question, for one of the principal difficulties in a study like history lies in recognizing the relevance of certain factors to certain other factors. Is it correct, for instance, to say that a particular type of economic structure in a given society is connected with a particular type of political constitution or religious organization? Part of the function of a scientific system or theory lies in its ability to co-ordinate and link together correlations between phenomena that have been observed to hold over immensely varying and diverse fields. An effect of this is to eliminate as *irrelevant* factors which, had the correlations been taken and viewed in isolation, might (conceivably) have been regarded as relevant. Thus factors involved in any particular case under examination may be rejected while others are taken into account by appealing to the organized and widely established body of knowledge that lies behind each individual inquiry undertaken by the scientist and which directs and governs the lines along which he pursues his investigation. This, to return to our crude example, is what makes it possible for the psychologist to 'see at a glance' that the month in which his patient was born is not a factor to be taken into account when he sets out to analyse his neurosis: and his ability to do this is in no way connected with a mysterious *a priori* intuition into the nature of the case before him.

The systematic character of a science, which enables the scientist to assert judgements of relevance often attaining to' a very high degree of precision, is of importance when science is contrasted with common sense. Commonsense generalizations obviously do assert a relevance existing between the phenomena they connect: that is a tautology. But they go no farther than this; they do not make a close structural analysis of the phenomena they roughly link together: they are content to notice a certain simple compresence or succession in experience, and that is all. In consequence, the explanations which they provide are of a vague and frequently unreliable kind, admitting of a multitude of exceptions. To take an elementary example, consider once again the difference between a medical explanation of why a person has caught pneumonia and a commonsense one. The ordinary man may explain it by saying that the sufferer stood too long in the cold and leave it at that. But he knows also that there are many instances of people standing in the cold and not catching pneumonia. His generalization is, therefore, of the form: other things being equal, people who stand too long in the cold contract pneumonia. And the question remains whether other things are in fact equal in the particular case. The medical specialist, on the other hand, is in a position to provide a far wider and more comprehensive account of the conditions favouring the contraction of pneumonia in a given instance; and the possibility of exceptions or counter-cases to his diagnoses has been correspondingly reduced. Yet the difference in the position of the ordinary man and the specialist remains essentially one of degree. For the latter can never be certain that in the case with which he is dealing he has taken into account all the relevant factors, that there may not have been hidden peculiarities of which he has failed to take account; and the ordinary man, as was pointed out above, is not 'wrong' in his explanation—he is not denying anything the specialist may assert regarding the action of bacteria upon the blood-stream and so forth. He is merely not in a position to make explicit the type of factors that are made explicit when the specialist analyses the case; and he therefore leaves room for the tabulation of these factors by inserting a wide *ceteris paribus* clause.

The creation of scientific systems, and the complex inter-relation between hypotheses of higher and lower levels of generality and abstraction, is accompanied by the development of corresponding terminologies. It is essential to grasp something of the nature and function of these terminologies if the generation of barren philosophical debates is to be avoided. These debates tend to arise in the following way. Scientists and ordinary people often seem to be talking about different things when they produce explanations of events. Where the ordinary person talks about tables and chairs, the scientist discusses neutrons and electrons; where the ordinary person talks about minds and 'nerves', the psycho-analyst discusses the unconscious and traumata. And the suspicion arises that the scientist is discussing entities lying upon a different level of existence, that he is describing the inhabitants of a rarefied world of which he is a privileged observer. But this may lead to confusion, and to the senseless reduplication of worlds.[1]

In a great many cases where scientists and ordinary people appear to be talking about different worlds in the same way, they are in fact talking about the same world in different ways. How does this come about? The answer lies in recognizing the purpose of conceptual systems. All descriptive concepts have some reference to past and future observations; a descriptive concept that did not meet this requirement would have no use. This does not, however, entail that concepts are all of the same type. As a science advances, new concepts are introduced and old ones subtly alter in meaning or disappear altogether. The evolution and change of the conceptual apparatus of a given science is an index of the development of that science.

The use of a scientific concept (like that of any other empirical concept) is determined by a specific range of observations, the nature and limits of this range being dictated by the practical requirements and the stage of development of the system in which it functions. For instance, the meaning of the term 'unconscious' when it occurs in psycho-analysis is ultimately to be understood in terms of the experiences and behaviour of individual human beings when these are considered in the context of psycho-analytical theory and technique. And the same dependence upon observational criteria is, of course, true of an everyday term like 'penny': the meaning of this word can only be grasped in terms of the conditions under which it is correct to use it, and these conditions will have reference to seeing and touching. Nor is this procedure any more mysterious when it is adopted by science than when it is adopted in common life. The 'things' science studies are originally the macroscopic objects of common sense. The 'things' it ends up with are not—it finishes by talking about

[1] See the well-known attack on Eddington in Stebbing's *Philosophy and the Physicists*.

electrons, unconscious minds, anticyclones, and so forth.
There is, however, no occasion for surprise; and to worry
about the reality of the entities scientific terms refer to on the
grounds that they are unobservable or not directly observable
is unnecessary.[1] Both everyday and scientific concepts refer
to 'things' in that in both cases certain correlations are made
part of their definition; they represent, as it were, landmarks
in the advance of knowledge. It is found that in a number of
cases phosphorus melts at 44° C. This begins as an empirical
law. Later, as science continues to develop, this law tends to
assume the form of an analytic proposition within the system,
and melting at 44° C. comes to be regarded as an essential
property of phosphorus. 'Thing-words' are used where certain
correlations have become analytic within a system, that is to
say, when it has been found convenient to treat certain properties as always occurring together; and consequently our
criterion for deciding whether a certain thing-word should be
applied in a particular case is whether the correlations
demanded by the definition of the thing-word that is in
question occur. We should not say that something we saw
was a chair if, when we tried to touch it, our hand passed
through the back of it. This is not to say that there are any
precise criteria for deciding when a chair is a chair and when
it is something else. The whole point about commonsense
concepts is their vagueness and their 'open texture';[2] we can
point to some of the ways in which we should justify our calling
something a chair and not something else, but there will
always remain a looseness and uncertainty about our use of
empirical concepts in everyday life. And in this, as was pointed
out early on, lies their utility.

When, however, we consider some scientific concepts an
important difference is noticeable. In psycho-analysis the

---

[1] It would be mistaken, however, to suggest that 'high-level' concepts of this
type are related to observations in the way in which everyday empirical concepts
are related to observations. For to understand the observational significance of
the former, we must understand the theories wherein they play an essential part.

[2] See F. Waismann, 'Verifiability', *Proceedings of the Aristotelian Society*,
supplementary vol. xix.

concepts used are admittedly similar in respect of looseness and vagueness to those of common sense, and that is perhaps a partial explanation why many of them slide without very much difficulty into ordinary discourse. Yet it is noteworthy that even within the sphere of psychology another school, the behaviourists, has emphasized the use of concepts which are more precise and which can be expressed in terms of measurement. And this is significant since it is a feature of what are called the 'advanced sciences' to use concepts of this kind. Thus, if it is asked what is meant by saying 'there is an electric current running through that wire', it will not be suggested in answer that there is literally an observable stream of electricity running along the wire like water down a pipe.[1] It will, on the other hand, be quite reasonable to say that it implies such statements as: 'If you touch the wire you will receive a shock', or: 'If you attach an electric light bulb to the end of the wire it will be illuminated', and so on. But there is another way whereby the meaning can be expressed, and it is in terms of a reading from an ammeter that not only records the presence or otherwise of the current, but also provides a measurement of its strength. And that is true of scientific concepts wherever measurement is possible. For quantitative measurement means the referring of the entity to be measured to a standard independent of the feelings of the observer—the varying sensations of the different people who receive a shock from touching the wire, for instance. Thus, wherever possible we find the scientist will choose as the definitions for his concepts those capable of being expressed in measurable terms. The advantages of this procedure are clear. Not only does it admit into scientific work an element of precision and objectivity lacking in purely qualitative studies, but, further, the introduction of numerical values makes it possible to use mathematical formulae and transformation-rules as a quick, convenient method of calculation and deduction within the scientific system. These features of a scientific language are

[1] Although this analogy is often used when electricity is being taught, in the present writer's experience it was far from being a helpful one.

indicative of the degree of systematization and development the science itself has attained.

We find, for example, that a law, as stated in physics, is not expressed in the form of ordinary crude generalizations like 'All men are mortal' or 'All water boils when heated', but in terms of formulae of functional dependence. And so, while it may be true to say that such a law connects phases of phenomena at a given time with phases of other phenomena at a given time, it is nevertheless not true to say that it is concerned merely to assert a simple correlation of a rather vague kind. Its distinctive characteristic is that it allows for an infinite number of possible values, and whichever of these we choose to substitute for the variable on one side of the formula will enable us to calculate with accuracy the value of the variable on the other side. In this way it is possible to deduce from a given formula taken in conjunction with certain data an infinitely wide range of values. In fact, almost all laws of physics have 'the form of equations in which some variable is a function of some other variable. For example, if x = the displacement of a body on an inclined plane, t = the time, then there is a function $5x = t^2$. This is a propositional function which yields a correspondence between values of x and values of t.'[1] What we find in physics is a functional correlation in terms of measurement that is different from the simple $(x)\phi x \supset \psi x$ type of correlation, in the sense that the former represents a generalization which is at once compendious and precise.

With this we may conclude our brief discussion of common-sense and scientific explanation, and in the light of what has been said consider the relationship between the two.

Russell was quoted as saying that physics had ceased to look for causes 'because there are no such things'. This is true so far as the physicist is concerned. But the term 'cause' is, as we saw, a function of a given language, and we do not, nor could we wish to, talk physics all the time. The ability to frame empirical laws in terms of functional formulae is

[1] R. Weinberg, *An Examination of Logical Positivism*, p. 148.

dependent upon the existence of a conceptual framework within which the terms used have an accepted definition in use of a measurable kind. But not all our terms are like this, nor, for reasons already given, would it be convenient for us if they were. The case with most of our words was best expressed by Hume when he wrote:

> . . . we do not annex distinct and complete ideas to every term we make use of, and . . . in talking of *government, church, negotiation, conquest,* we seldom spread out in our minds all the simple ideas of which these complex ones are composed. It is, however, observable, that notwithstanding this imperfection, we may avoid talking nonsense on these subjects, and may perceive any repugnance among the ideas as well as if we had a full comprehension of them. Thus, if instead of saying, that in war the vanquished have always recourse to negotiations, we should say, that they have always recourse to conquest, the custom which we have acquired of attributing certain relations to ideas, still follows the words, and makes us immediately perceive the absurdity of that proposition. . . .[1]

For in everyday life we do not demand precision, and these general terms serve the purposes of communication adequately. It is only when we begin to examine our subject-matter more closely, and, in the way that science does, look for wider and more precisely specifiable regularities in our experience, that our everyday concepts begin to raise difficulties which demand their change, or the substitution of different concepts. And this, when it is not recognized by the investigator, may produce confusion. As an illustration it is only necessary to glance at the work of a so-called 'scientific historian' like Spengler.[2] Spengler speaks confidently of 'cultures' having life-cycles; but it is not at all clear whether he intends this to be understood as an empirical law or as an analytic proposition. He frequently appears to choose his examples of 'cultures' according to the criterion ' "x is a culture" implies "x has a life-cycle",' in which case his assertion is *a priori*; at other times he seems anxious to regard his cultures as having other defining properties, and, using them as his data, to demon-

---

[1] Hume, *Treatise of Human Nature*, p. 31 (Everyman Edition).
[2] Oswald Spengler, *The Decline of the West*.

strate that they all, as a matter of empirical fact, have passed through the same phases of birth, growth, decay, and death. Dr. Arnold Toynbee's use of the term 'civilization' has often a similar ambiguity, but further consideration of this problem must be postponed until we come to analyse it in rather more detail later. Here it is sufficient to point out that these concepts, since they are not susceptible of quantitative interpretation and since their area of reference is so ill-defined, are often believed to require a special treatment, aptly termed by Professor Popper 'methodological essentialism',[1] which consists in an intuitive grasping of essences; this view entails the theory that, while it is true to say that scientific concepts are descriptive of how phenomena behave, concepts like 'civilization', and 'the State' refer to essences which remain the same however much their external manifestations may change.

The root of the trouble lies in not recognizing the nature of conceptual systems. A developing science accumulates new concepts and 'technical terms' in order to express correlations, discovered in the course of its advance, economically and fruitfully.[2] These concepts, since they are deliberately created by the scientist for the sake of convenience, tend to have an accepted definition within the system involved, although, as we have already noticed, some are interpreted more loosely than others. But it is dangerous to suppose that concepts like 'civilization' or 'culture', which have an exceedingly vague use in ordinary discourse, belong to the same category as these, or could be fitted into it with a very little trouble. Adapted originally to the needs of everyday speech, they will slip and slide when attempts are made to treat them 'scientifically', giving more help to the sophist and the charlatan than to the honest investigator.

It follows that the form taken by empirical laws, and hence

[1] K. R. Popper, 'The Poverty of Historicism', *Economica*, 1944–5.
[2] See R. von Mises, *Probability, Statistics and Truth*, p. 4. Von Mises writes: 'In the first place, the content of a concept (in the exact sciences) is not derived from the meaning popularly given to a word, and it is therefore independent of current usage. . . . In the second place, the value of a concept is not gauged by its correspondence with some usual group of notions, but only by its usefulness for further scientific development, and so indirectly for everyday affairs.'

the pattern of explanation in general, is relative to the conceptual framework involved. Where common sense is concerned, explanation naturally takes a causal form; and it is vain to try to make this more precise than common sense requires. Questions about the exact moment at which the cause ends and the effect begins, and endeavours to narrow both cause and effect down until each occupies a single instant, are due to a misunderstanding of the role of causality in ordinary discourse, and represent pointless attempts to assimilate the latter to scientific discourse.

To sum up. We do not find causal laws occurring in advanced sciences like physics, but this does not imply that causality has become in general otiose. It may be indispensable upon other levels. Nor does it imply that explanation in physics is of a wholly different order: the explanation of the physicist and the explanation of the 'plain man' both depend upon observed correlations in experience. And between the two are interposed those sciences whose terminologies have not attained the quantitative precision of physics, and which still have a use for causal forms of explanation. Finally, every individual explanation must be viewed and interpreted in relation to the context of inquiry within which it occurs, not merely criticized on the ground that it does not conform with some fixed and immutable Idea laid up in heaven. We may expect to find many common notions familiar to us in our everyday thinking recurring in the sciences, but we must not be surprised if we find them changed, like the faces of people we once knew, or even replaced altogether. The constructive task of the philosopher lies in sympathetic analysis rather than in justification and condemnation.

§ 3. *Some Additional Remarks*

IN the preceding sections explanation has been considered under what may loosely be termed its 'regularity' aspect. But the importance was stressed of distinguishing between the different descriptive contexts wherein explanatory terms may function, although this distinction must be handled cautiously.

It is mistaken, for example, to claim for scientific explanation a *superiority* over commonsense explanation: both have their use. We do not want to be scientists all the time. Indeed, to quarrel with a commonsense explanation on the ground that it lacks the precision and comprehensiveness of an explanation occurring in one of the sciences is to complain that it should perform a different function from the one it in fact performs, and this I have given reasons for supposing to be pointless.

There is one further point that should be made. From what has been said it may appear that every explanation of the above kind that is ever uttered always contains a reference to one or more generalizations. But the expression 'contain a reference' is ambiguous. It may well be argued that very often to give an ordinary causal explanation—'he slipped because he stepped on a banana skin'—does not seem to involve reference to a generalization, either for the speaker who enunciates the explanation or for the hearer who understands it. Such an objection may be circumvented by the device of saying that on such occasions only an *implicit* reference to a generalization is expressed. But the vagueness of the rider does not make it particularly illuminating.

It is a mistake to suppose that our daily life is wholly governed by a knowledge of general laws derived from past experience, which we 'apply' whenever we have to act. We should be surprised were it suggested that a man's walking confidently along the road was due to a belief held by him that, since the pavement had supported him upon all previous occasions, it would continue to support him now. Our normal activities are not eternally haunted and shadowed by general statements in this way; we tend to react habitually to a large number of types of situation; and it is only when somebody (a philosopher perhaps) asks questions like 'Why do you risk walking on the pavement—it *might* give way?' that we may justify our actions in terms of statements referring to past experiences.

The same thing is true of many of our ordinary explanations.

When we are told that the man next door sprained his ankle because he slipped on a banana skin we do not have to perform an imaginary act of looking through the bundle of generalizations at the back of our minds for one marked 'Slipping On Banana Skins' before we can understand the explanation presented to us. For the explanation convinces by appealing to our familiarity with certain sorts of situation, our 'knowing what to expect'.

This is important, because there is always a tendency to over-intellectualize the implications of our ordinary speech, and this in turn is liable to lead to the belief that much of our thinking and reasoning is more systematic and formalized than it really is. There are cases where, it is true, generalizations are brought out into the open, but on the commonsense level this is the exception rather than the rule, and it depends upon the complexity or recondite character of the explanation provided. For instance, if someone informs me that he is being given penicillin because he has pneumonia and I say (in surprise) 'I didn't know they gave penicillin for pneumonia' or 'Does penicillin cure pneumonia, then?', the generalization is brought into the open, and what was taken for granted by the sufferer is made explicit by my remark.

What has been said does not, of course, conflict with our general analysis of causal connexion. For whenever a causal *explanation* is doubted or queried (as opposed to the doubting or querying of the truth-value of one of its limbs—'did he *really* tread on a banana skin?') it is the generalization that warrants its utterance which comes under fire, and the same generalization must be defended by reference to previous experience if the claim to have offered a satisfactory explanation is to be upheld. In this sense it may be correct to speak of an 'implicit' reference to generalizations in all explanations.

It may be asked what bearing all that has been said about the nature of scientific and commonsense explanation has upon the problem of historical explanation. The answer will, I hope, become clear in what is to follow. For it is, I think, a feature of much written on this subject that too little attention has been paid to the flexibility of the notion of causal explanation in general, and that there has been a corresponding tendency to be impressed (and obsessed) exclusively by scientific explanation. My object will be to indicate the relationship between historical explanations and other forms of explanation, bringing out the differences, it is true, but trying not to forget that there may be points in common.

PART II

THE SUBJECT-MATTER OF HISTORY

§ 1. *The Argument that History is* Sui Generis

THE argument of the first part of this book was concerned with an examination of the nature of explanation as it frequently occurs upon the levels of common sense and the sciences, and the extent to which it may be analysed in terms of regularity. In this and the succeeding part we shall be concerned with the question of how far it is legitimate to extend this type of analysis into the field of historical explanation and how far such analysis is capable of shedding light upon the problem of historical explanation in general.

Many arguments have been put forward at various times, claiming that analysis of this kind is impossible within the sphere of history, and condemning attempts to introduce it as wrong-headed and doomed to failure. These arguments are of two forms, a weaker and a stronger. The weaker admits the importance of causality, for instance, as a category of historical thought, but denies that it has the function in history that it has elsewhere.[1] The stronger questions the place of causality in history altogether, suggesting that historical explanation has its own unique categories.

The foundation of these views lies in the theory that the subject-matter of history is different in kind from the subject-matter of those studies loosely called the 'natural sciences'. History is a different 'mode of experience', and the historian must in consequence approach it with methods entirely distinct from the methods of the natural scientist; in history the scientist's inductive and experimental techniques, his classificatory approach to his material, are out of place and are simply not to be found. To understand history and the writing of it the scientific conception of knowledge must be discarded,

---

[1] See the chapter, ' "Cause" in History', in R. G. Collingwood's *Metaphysics*; and also the same author's *Idea of History*, p. 214.

and a distinct type of knowledge must be recognized: this
type of knowledge has been variously named—it is termed
sometimes 'insight', sometimes 'intuition' or 'empathy', and
sometimes 'recreating past experience' (Collingwood) or
're-experiencing somebody else's thought' (Dilthey's 'das
Nacherleben').[1] This form of knowledge is appropriate to
history, and it is the *only* appropriate form of knowledge. The
following quotations from the two works just mentioned make
this clear:

> Historical knowledge is the knowledge of what mind has done in the
> past, and at the same time it is the redoing of this, the perpetuation of
> past acts in the present. Its object is therefore not a mere object, some-
> thing outside the mind which knows it; it is an activity of thought,
> which can be known only in so far as the knowing mind re-enacts it and
> knows itself as so doing. To the historian, the activities whose history
> he is studying are not spectacles to be watched, but experiences to be
> lived through in his own mind.[2]
>
> Mankind, if apprehended only by perception and perceptual know-
> ledge, would be for us a physical fact, and as such it would be accessible
> only to natural-scientific knowledge. It becomes an object for the human
> studies only in so far as they find expression in living utterances, and
> in so far as those expressions are understood. Of course this relationship
> of life, expression and understanding embraces not only the gestures,
> looks, and words in which men communicate. . . . The mind-body unit
> of life is known to itself through the same double relationship of lived
> experience and understanding.[3]

It is clear that, given this approach to the problem of historical knowledge, any attempt to assimilate historical explanation
to the types of explanation so far studied would be, to say the
least, superficial and misleading, a distortion of the nature of
historical thinking. But are we compelled to accept this interpretation and all its implications? Does there really exist this
clear-cut and unbridgeable cleavage between history and other
forms of knowledge, or has the contrast between the two been
over-emphasized? Can we set the distinction between them

---

[1] See H. A. Hodges, *Wilhelm Dilthey: an Introduction*, p. 160.
[2] R. G. Collingwood, *The Idea of History*, p. 218.
[3] Wilhelm Dilthey, *The Construction of the Historical World in the Human
Studies*; the passage in question is quoted by H. A. Hodges, op. cit., p. 142.

in a clearer light, and by so doing recognize the affinities as well as the differences in their respective methods of explanation?

What is meant by saying that 'history is autonomous', and that 'the world of history' is not 'the world of science'? There are various grounds upon which this proposition has been maintained by philosophers, many of which are unsatisfactory. For example, it may be affirmed as an *a priori* self-evident truth; everyone in his senses can see that history is 'different' and, if there are those who cannot, then it is so much the worse for them. But the criterion of self-evidence here, as always, introduces an undesirable subjectivity into the matter. Alternatively, it appears sometimes to be suggested that the autonomous nature of history follows from the impossibility of assimilating historical explanation to ordinary causal explanation. The principle that historical events are causally connected in the sense that the statement of such a connexion entails a reference to laws or generalizations does not constitute a presupposition of the historian's interpretation of historical change: according to Professor Oakeshott[1] there are no general laws in history by means of which individual historical events can be 'reduced to instances of a principle'. The historian applies his own categories to his material, and, in so far as he uses the causal category at all, he uses it in an especial sense, the sense defined by Collingwood where 'cause' in history is always to be understood as referring to 'the thought in the mind of the person by whose agency the event came about' this being 'not something other than the event' but 'the inside of the event itself'.[2] But this argument is also open to exception, since, when it is asked why it is impossible to assimilate historical to ordinary causal explanation, the answer seems frequently to be that this must be so in virtue of the nature of historical knowledge, and hence it cannot be used without circularity to justify the theory that history is *sui generis*.

[1] See Michael Oakeshott, *Experience and its Modes*, p. 161.
[2] *The Idea of History*, pp. 214–15.

There is, nevertheless, much to recommend the distinction thus drawn between history and science. Although there is an air of mystery about some of its pronouncements, this does not detract from its importance as countering the belief that the historian is really a kind of scientist in spite of his outlandish garb, and that if we only take the trouble to tear off enough of his disguises we shall find the genuine article underneath. What is not so clear and is more difficult to accept, is the proposition that the 'world of experience' treated by the historian is a self-contained world that must accordingly be interpreted by methods bearing little or no relation to those used in other branches of knowledge. For to say this is apparently to say something very much stronger than a simple denial of the truth of the assertion that history is a science, no less and no more. And we must ask whether it is not possible to retain the autonomy of history as a branch of study, while at the same time escaping from the division of human experience into sharply differentiated worlds, and consequently avoiding the view that our knowledge must be locked up into rigid, water-tight compartments.[1]

It is desirable to do this, because the theory of the autonomy of history as it stands leads to paradoxical results. It would be hard to convince the average practising historian that the events he describes are in some sense peculiar, that they are not capable of investigation by the scientist or susceptible to generalization by the 'plain man'. He would be surprised (I think) if he were informed that he did not use the word 'cause' very much as it is used by everybody else, and bewildered if we put it to him that the 'facts of history are present facts' and that history is 'the continuous assertion of a past which is not past, and a present which is not present' (Oakeshott), that 'all history is the history of thought' (Collingwood) and hence that 'all history is contemporary history' (Croce), because, since historical events can constantly be rethought, they are not 'in time'.

---

[1] Cf. Oakeshott: 'History, like every other form of experience, must make its material as well as determine its method, for the two are inseparable.' Op. cit., p. 90.

This kind of description of the historian's activity is confusing because it gives the impression that the historian, however much he may imagine that what he is concerned with is things that once 'really happened', albeit in the past, is only talking about ideas floating about like bubbles on the surface of his mind.[1] It may be argued that that is not at all the model philosophers who have talked in this way have had before them, that we are deliberately misunderstanding their terminology. But we may justifiably answer that, if such is the case, their terminology is misleading and the point they want to emphasize might be less confusingly expressed. And that is precisely what I wish to do.

The philosophy of history tends to fall between two extremes. At one extreme lies the view that history is a branch of knowledge which is *sui generis*: at the other, there is the claim that it is, in some sense, a department of science or, at any rate, that it is capable of being transformed into such a department. Both of these views, taken in isolation, lead to difficulties; yet both, I believe, are important. For the philosophers who say that history is *sui generis* are stressing those features of the methods, aims, and subject-matter of the historian which lead us to discriminate between history and the natural sciences. And the philosophers who insist that history is 'really scientific' stress those features of the subject which lead us into regarding it as upon all fours with natural science.

In the sections that follow I shall suggest that there is truth in both the contending doctrines. In particular I shall examine those characteristics of historical writing and thinking which have been considered to be the most formidable obstacle to attempts to assimilate historical explanation to explanation as it occurs in the sciences. I shall argue that the examination of the features in question certainly precludes the possibility of a wholesale assimilation, but that nevertheless it does not

---

[1] History is said by Oakeshott to form 'a world of ideas', which it is the historian's business to 'create and construct'. See *Experience and Its Modes*, p. 90. Cf. also Croce's insistence upon the contemporaneity of all history.

force us to draw the inference that the historian's field of study is in a mysterious way distinct from the world of the scientist or of the ordinary person, that it is set ontologically apart, and that it 'dictates' to the historian a different technique of description and interpretation. For, in the first place, I do not know what it means to say that a field of study 'dictates', unless this is merely another way of expressing the fact that we choose our methods of research within any area of inquiry according to the purposes we have in mind. And, in the second place, I assume that the historian, the scientist, and the ordinary person inhabit a common world. It may be objected that this is a 'metaphysical statement': I should prefer to call it a 'methodological principle', defensible on the grounds that its consequences for philosophy are less paradoxical than others which allow for the multiplication of separate worlds. Hence my aim will be to try to show that the differences between history and other branches of inquiry may be accounted for, not on grounds that necessitate the postulation of such worlds, but on other grounds connected with the purposes of historical research, and with the methods and the conceptual frameworks appropriate to those purposes.

In this manner it may be possible to clear the ground, and to remove unwarranted encumbrances, whether these be soap-bubble theories of separate spheres of existence, or cast-iron prejudices about the scientific character of all knowledge. And then, when this has been done and when it is taken in conjunction with what was said in Part I, we may proceed to look at historical explanation afresh and consider the historian's causal statements and their relations to the explanatory statements occurring in other fields without having to take into account the objections that our inquiry is (a) irrelevant, since 'cause' is not a fundamental category of historical explanation, (b) misleading, since 'cause' has a totally different meaning in history from its meaning in scientific or ordinary discourse. And, while it will be recognized that there is no single, privileged usage of 'cause' in history, nevertheless it will be seen that it has usages therein which are closely related to its usages in common speech, and that this connexion sheds light upon the problem of the relationship between history and science.

The four propositions often put forward in support of the theory that history is an autonomous branch of study, irreducible in principle to any other, are the following:

- A. Historical events are past events and hence cannot be known in the manner in which present events are known.
- B. Historical events are unique and unclassifiable.
- C. History describes the actions, statements, and thoughts of human beings, not the behaviour of 'dead matter' with which science is concerned.
- D. Historical events have an irreducible richness and complexity.

These propositions will now be examined in turn.

§ 2. *Is There a Problem about the Past?*

The so-called 'problem of past events' has been a frequent bone of contention amongst philosophers, and there is not space to enter into its various ramifications here. But that it has a particular relevance to questions relating to the philosophy of history is clear from the obvious fact that history is essentially the study of the past; and, furthermore, as Professor Field has rightly emphasized, it is a presupposition of all historical thought 'that what happened in the past is absolutely independent of our present thinking about it'.[1] Professor Field goes on to say that 'the assumption that something happened' is a 'synthetic *a priori* proposition'; if by the latter it is meant that 'it is constitutive of our sense of the only reality by reference to which empirical judgements could have either truth or falsity or any meaning at all',[2] this is certainly correct.[3]

---

[1] 'Some Problems of the Philosophy of History', *British Academy Annual Philosophical Lecture*, 1938.

[2] C. I. Lewis, *An Analysis of Knowledge and Valuation*, p. 361.

[3] The use of the word 'assumption' in this context seems to me to be a questionable one, however. I feel even less happy about the notion of *existential* synthetic *a priori* statements.

Past events have, nevertheless, caused philosophers worry, although the remedies they have proposed as cures for this worry have, as so often, proved worse than the disease. For they have ended by producing theories of the past which amount to a denial of the legitimacy of speaking of past events as opposed to present events at all, and which thus destroy the validity of the assumption they originally set out to justify. How does this come about?

The nature of the initial difficulty may be stated as follows:

When we discuss events in the past it is true by definition that we are not directly acquainted with them. But, it is argued, I can only correctly be said to know an event when I am actually observing it: true knowledge is knowledge by acquaintance. In what sense, then, can I be said to know an event which is in principle unobservable, having vanished behind the mysterious frontier which divides the present from the past? And how can we be sure that anything ever really happened in the past at all, that the whole story is not an elaborate fabrication, as untrustworthy as a dream or a work of fiction? The net result has been for philosophers to assume that there is something radically suspect or 'wrong' about statements referring to the past. Yet we do, and apparently must, make them.

Confronted with this dilemma, philosophers have proposed odd solutions. For instance, they have resorted to the expedient of saying that the events with which, for example, historians deal are not past but present.[1] According to Oakeshott, the historian's 'world of experience' 'ends but does not begin with facts'. The correspondence theory of history is impossible because the facts with which history books are alleged to correspond are outside experience and consequently unknowable. 'If the historical past be knowable, it must belong to the present world of experience; if it be unknowable, history is worse than futile, it is impossible' he writes in *Experience and Its Modes*, p. 107. The past 'varies with the present, rests

---

[1] It has also been suggested that statements about the past are really hypotheses for the prediction of *future* experiences.

upon the present, is the present'; and, in support of this last proposition, he says that the expression 'what really happened' must be replaced by the expression 'what the evidence obliges us to believe'.

Those passages are significant not only because they rightly point to a confusion about the nature of historical facts to which we shall have to return (Part III, § 2), but also because they are indicative of the nature of the philosopher's worry about the pastness of historical events. For this is disclosed to be a dissatisfaction with the past for not being present.[1]

Yet it is surely curious to demand that it should be. And the reason for the demand seems to lie in the pre-eminent status allotted to 'knowledge by acquaintance' as the ideal type of cognition. This must now be examined.

What is 'knowledge by acquaintance'? In ordinary speech, 'I know such-and-such a thing by acquaintance' means the same as 'I am acquainted with such-and-such a thing'. And we do not speak of being acquainted with events. We do not even, as a rule, speak of being acquainted with things. The expression is reserved principally for places, books, languages, and, in particular, persons. We can speak of 'knowing a language' or 'knowing a person' where 'knowing' entails 'being acquainted with'. But we do not normally speak of 'knowing a table' or 'knowing a hammer' (although we *may* do so, if, for instance, we wish to say that we know that, if care is not taken, the table may collapse, or that we know the best way of using the hammer). Likewise, do we speak of 'knowing a flash of lightning' or 'knowing the outbreak of a war'? The point about certain usages of the verb 'to know' is that in such usages it is followed by a proposition, and that this use of the verb is quite different from those uses where it takes a direct object, a distinction that must be kept in mind when we are concerned with knowing what happened in the past or in history.

---

[1] Croce speaks of history as 'knowledge of the *eternal present*' (*Theory and History of Historiography*, p. 61). It is not easy to regard this as being other than self-contradictory.

Let us imagine that I say that I know that I went to the pillar-box this morning to post a letter. Somebody asks me how I know. I may answer him in various ways. I may say that I have a distinct memory of having done so; I may point to the fact that the letter is no longer in my room; I may even produce a witness who affirms that he saw me drop the letter into the pillar-box. By such methods, I can produce credentials to substantiate my claim to knowledge of a particular portion of my biography. And a point will come when my questioner will be forced to admit that I have succeeded in establishing my claim. What he will not do is to demand the logically impossible, namely, ask me to point to some event in the past with which I am acquainted when I say that I know that I posted the letter this morning. Thus, to say that we know that such-and-such an event occurred in the past is, in a way, to stake a claim, the claim that, if asked to produce conclusive reasons to justify our statement, we shall be able to do so.

This fact throws some light upon the problem of 'the reality of the past', the scepticism often expressed about it, and the tendency, noted above, to assimilate past events to dream events, fictitious events, and so forth. The word 'real' has a fatal ambiguity. 'Real' is used in so many different ways that it would be futile to attempt to enumerate them all; the important point is to recognize that it has many different usages, and that to call something 'real' is not to do so in virtue of some common quality 'stamped' upon all the various things to which it is applied.

Now, while there are clear senses in which it is correct to speak of events as being 'real' or 'unreal', these senses are quite separate from the present–past distinction. We may say: 'Is there really a war taking place in South America at the moment?' and we may say: 'Did this event really happen?' The criteria for deciding the reality or otherwise of an event are not criteria of tense. And the supposition that they may be is possibly derived from viewing reality as a single common 'property' in the manner described above.[1] Taking as a model

[1] Cf. the contribution by J. L. Austin to the symposium 'Other Minds',

those cases where to say that something does not exist is equivalent to saying that it is unreal[1] (objects and places in dreams, characters in novels, &c.) we may be led to suppose that this use is exhaustive of all contexts. But such a view leads to confusions. It is, of course, precisely to distinguish past events from dreams, fictions, and so forth, that we use the word 'real' with regard to them. And we have certain specifiable criteria for making this distinction. These criteria involve the production of evidence and witnesses as an assurance that what is described as having taken place has not been 'made up' or dreamt. And, again, we do not require that the event in question should be observable here and now: this requirement would have to be met if, and only if, it were a present event that was being referred to and not a past one.

Thus, questions about the reality of all past events and the possibility of our knowing them tend to be as misleading as the answers to them are unfortunate. It is, of course, true that not all philosophers have gone as far as Oakeshott in denying the validity of historical knowledge unless it be knowledge of the present. Other solutions have been provided, less extreme, but nevertheless on the same lines.

Some of these seem to be connected with the fact that spatial metaphors are often employed to talk about the past. Not only do we speak of things happening '*in* the past' (compare the way we describe our psychical experience—'in the mind', 'deep down within him') but we often hear people saying, for instance, 'let us cast our eyes back over the panorama of the past'. Such expressions arouse the idea that past events subsist in a mysterious world of their own. It is felt that, if only we could visit this world, all would be well and we should return with incontestable knowledge of what goes on there. Unfortunately, however, we are not able to do this, and our knowledge can be at best fragmentary and defective.

This might be called 'The Time-Machine Fallacy'; and,

Proceedings of the Aristotelian Society, supplementary vol. xxi, for a general discussion of the ambiguity of 'real'.

[1] See G. E. Moore, 'The Conception of Reality', *Philosophical Studies,* particularly pp. 200, 201.

although no one, so far as I know, has ever explicitly maintained such a view of the past, I think that it has had an influence. It is insidious because the spatial model suggests that the past is still the present, albeit in a rarefied 'subsistent' form. And this, in its turn, gives rise to the belief that at any rate some aspects of the past survive and that it is possible to get into direct touch with these. It may be a travesty of Professor Collingwood's theories to suppose that he had any such picture in mind when he talked of the past interpenetrating the present and being 'incapsulated' within it, and when he wrote: 'It is not only the object of thought that somehow stands outside time; the act of thought does so, too; in this sense at least, that one and the same act of thought may endure through a lapse of time and revive after a time when it has been in abeyance.'[1] But the suggestion of some sort of telepathic communication with past thoughts is too insistent to be entirely disregarded. What is at least fairly clear is that in much of Collingwood's work the desire to assimilate the past to the present so that the requirements of the acquaintance theory of knowledge may be satisfied is in evidence.

However much the above views may have been criticized it is true that they bring out important features of historical writing. One of these is that our knowledge of the historical past is constructed out of evidence which is present here and now to our senses. Whether this evidence is documentary or archaeological it can be seen and touched. But it is not therefore legitimate to confuse the evidence for a past event, which is admittedly present, with the event for which it is evidence, when this is past. Yet this, as we have seen, has been done.[2]

Another point raised by such discussions is the fact that historical events are not repeatable. We are not able to confirm

---

[1] *The Idea of History*, p. 287.

[2] A related confusion is illustrated in early 'positivistic' discussions of the *meaning* of historical statements. According to a strict application of the verification-principle, it was argued, every statement about the past is equivalent to a statement about records, documents, &c. This argument is examined by Professor Ryle in an article 'Unverifiability-by-me' (*Analysis*, Oct. 1936). See also G. E. M. Anscombe, 'The Reality of the Past', in *Philosophical Analysis*, edited by Max Black (Cornell University Press).

a hypothesis that a given event occurred as the outcome of another specified event, or set of events, by making an experiment under laboratory conditions. (This restriction is not, of course, confined to history: it characterizes, for example, geology or philology.) We cannot reproduce what we believe to have been the conditions that determined the collapse of the Roman Empire and then watch for the consequences, in the fashion in which we can combine certain chemicals and then see whether the result agrees or disagrees with a prediction of the result of such a combination. And this, so it seems to me, points to a genuinely distinctive feature of the subject-matter and consequently the methodology of the historian as compared to that of certain of the natural sciences, a feature that is at least *connected* with the pastness of historical events.[1]

Such characteristics of historical knowledge must of course be respected by any account of historical explanation. But they need not by themselves involve the introduction of a bogus mysticism about the past.

§ 3. *Uniqueness in History*

'ALL characteristics of history', writes Croce at one point, 'can be reduced to the . . . identification of history with the individual judgement.'[2] In spite of its cryptic appearance, the meaning of this assertion is fairly clear.

History is about what happened on particular occasions. It is not about what usually happens or what always happens under certain circumstances; for this we go to science. It is about what did actually happen at a clearly specified period of time, in all its detail and in the context of what preceded it and of what succeeded it. The historian concentrates upon the event in its *unique individuality*, regarding it, not as an instance of a type, not as a member of a class, but as something which is to be viewed for and in itself. And this interest

---

[1] Although the difficulty is not, of course, derived from their pastness as such, but from the problem of reproducing present events sufficiently like them.

[2] *Logic*, section iii, pp. 279 ff.

in events for and in themselves is regarded as a distinguishing feature of historical writing. To quote Croce again: 'The vision of the thing done is necessary and is the sole *source* of history.'

This contention seems to be broadly correct: unfortunately conclusions have been drawn from it which are less defensible. For it is inferred that the uniqueness of the events studied by the historian excludes the possibility of their being classified or generalized about in any way. 'Uniqueness' is regarded as a quality which historical events possess; any attempt to subsume them under a general rule, to assimilate them to other events of a similar kind, is to sin against the nature of historical fact. Historical events must be 'intuited': in this process their essential individuality is grasped, although Croce, for example, admits that such intuition must be 'penetrated by the concept in its universality, particularity and singularity'. He sets the 'subject' against the 'predicate' in historical narration, terming the latter the 'logical element'. By isolating a genuine document, he says, something can be intuited and transformed into the subject of an individual judgement. And in such a judgement we are enabled to say, not only that the something intuited existed, but also, by virtue of the predicate of the judgement, what that something was.

What the above argument might amount to is this: an historical judgement has as its subject some word or phrase with individual and unique reference; it may refer to an event, as, e.g., in 'the Norman Conquest occurred in 1066', or it may equally refer to a person or thing, as, e.g., in 'Louis XVIII ascended the French throne in 1815'. In order to grasp or 'cognize' the uniqueness of any such person or event the special faculty of intuition is required; and hence 'intuition' comes to refer to the capacity the historian has for apprehending the unique element in his subject-matter. Croce, however, admits that things 'do not speak for themselves', and this is where the conceptual or logical aspect of our thinking is needed. And it is certainly true that historical writing requires both an intuitive and a conceptual element, if by this it is meant that it is not merely an uninterpreted agglomeration of symbols without reference to experience. History is an empirical study, and it is hence tautologically true that it has such reference. We cannot, however, say anything informative unless we use language, and language involves the classification of the 'given'. Intuitions without concepts are blind.

Croce, however, in emphasizing the unique element in historical judgement, seems to mean more than just this when he speaks of history as 'the narration of individual reality' and contrasts it with the natural sciences.[1] And it is made clearer, I think, what this 'more' is, when we find him saying that history is concerned with 'representations' which are 'individual', and, again, that the intuitive faculty essential to historical research is bound up with (equivalent to?) 'living again' past events. The unique simply *is* that which is intuited, that with which we are directly acquainted, and thus 'knowledge by acquaintance' once more emerges as the true goal of historical knowledge.[2] To grasp the individual and unique character of his subject-matter, the historian must re-experience the event that concerns him within his own mind.

There will be more to say of this in the next section. Here the point at issue is whether our recognizing that the historian's job is to describe and explain what happened upon specified occasions also involves our believing that historical events possess some absolute uniqueness which necessitates their being known and explained in an especial way.

As has been said, the model is again 'knowledge by acquaintance'. It is the model in this case because it is felt that it is by direct acquaintance, and by direct acquaintance alone, with what is happening that we truly grasp the full individuality of a particular situation. We see two red things and we call them 'red'; but our so naming them slurs over important differences between the two colours we perceive that are not

---

[1] These are described (curiously) as an 'aggregate of cognitions, arbitrarily abstracted and fixed' (*Aesthetic*, p. 30), and as concerned with 'representative concepts, which are not intuitions but spiritual formations of a practical nature'.

[2] See *Logic*, p. 3, where sensation is described as 'something active and cognitive, or as a cognitive act'.

reflected in our description of them. Everything is subtly different from every other thing. Everything is unique.

But such uniqueness, the uniqueness of inexpressible 'qualia', is without sense for the historian, as it is for anybody else who uses language. When an historian says that an event is unique, his statement is incomplete until he states in what respects it is unique. The attribution of the term 'unique' to any event or thing logically presupposes prior classification.

Thus, while it is true that the historian is interested in the unique, in order to bring out the individuality of that upon which his interest is focused he must describe in words those of its features that differentiate it from other things. It is, of course, the case that there must be something before us, something must be, if the expression is preferred, 'intuited', before this process of differentiation and separation can begin. But 'intuition' or sense-perception is only prior in this case in the sense that it is prior in every case where language is being used descriptively.

I conclude therefore (1) that uniqueness is not a mysterious simple quality possessed by some events as opposed to others, (2) that the (true) assertion that the historian is interested in events in their unique individuality in no way entails the view that the description or explanation of the events in question is of a peculiar kind, involving an especial, and in some sense primary, use of intuition. On the contrary, to say that something is unique is to describe some feature or features belonging to it (perceived or 'intuited') and not belonging to other things. Louis XIV was unique in the sense that he ruled over France at a particular period of her history, but he was not unique in being a man, nor was he unique in being a man who lived at a particular period. The Norman Conquest was unique in the sense that it occurred at a particular time and place, but it was not unique in the sense that events like it, the invasion of one country by another, for instance, have occurred on several occasions throughout history.

Once these points are recognized, certain connected problems vanish. For example, we need no longer take seriously the view that, since the historian is interested in unique events, his subject-matter is, *on these grounds*, incapable of being classified or generalized about. The given is neutral; and our judgements of uniqueness or otherwise depend amongst other things upon human selection, points of view, purposes, and convenience. We are at liberty to admit that in fact the historian is only concerned with describing past events and indicating how and why they occurred when they did. We may, too, agree that if someone used past events merely to illustrate certain laws of human behaviour which in turn could be used to predict possible future behaviour by human beings, then he was not, properly speaking, an historian but something else. And it is true that people who appear to be trying to do this kind of thing (Spengler, for instance, or Toynbee), make us chary of calling them historians. Such views may be allowed, but they in no way involve the supposition that there is some inherent quality of uniqueness in the events treated by historians which makes them in principle incapable of being treated as instances of generalizations; nor do they involve the complementary claim that when an historian sets out to explain a certain historical event he must needs do it in a fashion that does not involve reference to ordinary causal laws.

Historians tell us about the Massacre of St. Bartholomew's Day in particular rather than about massacres in general, and about the reasons for Henry II's quarrel with Becket in particular rather than the reasons for State and Church dissension in general. In a like manner, an historian may preface a work inquiring into, say, the causes of the French Revolution by mentioning the causes of revolutions in general; he may do this as a guide to show the reader the kind of factors he is looking out for throughout his investigation. He may point out that history shows that revolutions do not occur suddenly, from the blue, but that their occurrence is the result of a process which has been in motion for a long time, largely unnoticed both by contemporaries and by other historians who have dealt with the subject in its more 'superficial' aspects.

And he may go on to examine the history of France during the hundred years preceding the revolution in an attempt to bring to light the profound underlying causes. But he will be concerned throughout primarily with the French Revolution, and there will be no question of his treating of it with the principal aim of discovering its affinities to other revolutions, or of utilizing his findings to support his initial hypothesis concerning the causes of revolutions in general. The latter purpose is implicit in the writings of Marx and his successors, and it is on account of this that we perhaps feel a pang of doubt when we hear even so trenchant a piece of social analysis as Marx's *Eighteenth Brumaire of Louis Bonaparte* being called 'history'.[1]

The engineer is concerned with building particular bridges. The architect is concerned with designing particular houses. Like the engineer and the architect, the historian is concerned with reconstructing particular situations in the past. But, just as neither the architect nor the engineer is free to ignore the laws of mechanics in his work, so, I shall argue, the historian, for all his attention to the individual and the unique, is not free to disregard general laws in his work of reconstruction.

What has been said in this section should nevertheless not be misunderstood. It is not suggested, for instance, that Croce (amongst others) is not right in maintaining that, because the historian is interested principally in what happened in the particular case, it is important that he should try to articulate its elements in the fullest possible way and in the greatest detail. To this end the method of 'living again' the action or set of actions may be of considerable importance. But the extent to which we regard something as unique, or as an instance of a type, is a function of our interest. While to bring out to the full the individuality of a specified human action may involve 'rethinking it in the living dialectic of its genesis' (to borrow a phrase from Croce), this feature of the historian's

---

[1] Not the only reason: it is also suspected (with some justice) of being propagandist. Croce's remarks on this aspect of historical writing are illuminating. Cf. his *Theory and History of Historiography*, pp. 83 ff. 'History', he writes, never metes out justice, but always justifies.'

procedure is not 'dictated', or made necessary, by the uniqueness or the individuality of the historian's material in any mysterious sense. Nor, as Croce seems partly to suggest (although the obscurity of his exposition makes it difficult to attribute a definite view to him with any degree of assurance), is it the case that the attribution of uniqueness is made simply in virtue of 'intuition', or 'direct contact with the thing that happened' (*Logic*, p. 280). Sensory experience is no more, and no less, essential to the 'individual judgements' of the historian than it is to, say, the classificatory and general statements of the natural scientist.

§ 4. *The 'Inside–Outside' Theory of Historical Events*

THE view of the nature of the historian's subject-matter that must now be examined represents the most impressive argument used to support the contention that history is *sui generis*, and hence, by implication, that historical explanation is so also. Because of its importance it will not be treated in detail in this short section: such treatment must be reserved until Part IV. It does, however, appear true to say that the form in which it has frequently been presented is profoundly misleading. This, in its main outline, must first be stated.

On p. 213 of *The Idea of History*, Collingwood writes:

The historian, investigating any event in the past, makes a distinction between what may be called the outside and the inside of an event. By the outside of an event I mean anything belonging to it which can be described in terms of bodies and their movements. . . . By the inside of an event I mean that in it which can only be described in terms of thought. . . . The historian is never concerned with either of these to the exclusion of the other. He is investigating not mere events (where by a mere event I mean one which has only an outside and no inside) but actions, and an action is the unity of the outside and the inside of an event . . . he must always remember that . . . his main task is to think himself into this action, to discover the thought of its agent.

And again on p. 215 we find the following said:

The processes of nature can therefore be properly described as sequences of mere events, but those of history cannot. They are not processes of mere events but processes of actions, which have an inner side, consisting of processes of thought; and *what the historian is looking for is these processes of thought*. All history is the history of thought. [Italics mine.]

There are two principal points to be noted in the above passages. (1) There is the emphasis upon the difference between history and natural science; (2) there is the assertion that this difference consists in the fact that the historian is concerned with thoughts and not with the physical 'manifestations' of those thoughts. Once again, it is held that history may be distinguished from other studies by the nature of historical subject-matter.

However true it may be that human emotion and behaviour exhibit regularities of occurrence in situations of a certain type, and however much psychology may be able to produce hypotheses concerning such regularities, it is not the case that we always do, or always want to, explain human behaviour merely by referring to general hypotheses of this kind. For we view human behaviour not only in its reactive aspects, but also under the aspects of being purposive, calculated, planned. And we must agree that the distinction formulated in the above terms between history and science holds good in so far as we do not explain the movement of a 'piece of matter' by referring to its intention, whereas we may explain a human action by making such a reference. Nor do we talk about 'pieces of matter' having reasons or being motivated.

Granted that all this is true, I nevertheless contend that many formulations of this point, including that quoted from Collingwood, tend to be both artificial and misleading. Artificial, because we do not, for example, talk of human actions having 'insides' and 'outsides': the distinction is normally put in terms of what was done and why it was done. Misleading, because the introduction of a spatial metaphor gives the impression that what are called the 'insides' of events are queer objects, invisible engines that make the wheels go round. And it is only too easy to move from this to the supposition that, in order to 'know' the insides of historical events (where 'knowing' is knowing by acquaintance) some peculiar technique for looking at these is required, analogous to the use by bacteriologists and astronomers of microscopes and telescopes, although, of course, at the same time subtly different. Thus a picture is presented which depicts the historian as a man who examines difficult, recalcitrant entities —thoughts and intentions, plans and 'mental processes'—by means of 'intuition', 're-enactment of past experience', and so forth. In Collingwood's words: 'to know someone else's activity of thinking is possible only on the assumption that this same activity can be re-enacted in one's own mind' (op. cit., p. 288).

Now this is a curious picture and it leads to a great deal of trouble, not least for Collingwood himself. After criticizing Dilthey on the ground that he 'conceives history in terms of psychology' (p. 173), he reaches the conclusion, previously quoted, that 'it is not only the object of thought that stands outside time; the act of thought does so, too: in this sense, at least, that one and the same act of thought may endure through a lapse of time and revive after a time when it has been in abeyance' (p. 287). In this way, the subject-matter of the historian has not merely been increased: as well as 'thoughts' he must deal with 'objects of thought' (and so also, presumably, with 'objects of intention', 'objects of planning', &c.). A new *attribute* has been added to these entities, the attribute of timelessness, which apparently permits the thinker to 'partake' of them whenever he makes the effort.

What is confusing here is the assimilation of so-called 'mental events' to 'things' in the everyday sense of the word. It is an irony of Collingwood's treatment of the problem that, after insisting (rightly) upon the distinction between the ordinary, 'physical' furniture of the world, and our thoughts, intentions, and so forth, he ends by reaching a position not so far from that which he is legitimately attacking. And the net result is to produce a theory of the subject-matter of history wherein the 'insides' of historical events are held to be like the physical events happening around us—a man crossing the road, a child going to school—yet different, in the sense that they cannot be seen, touched, or heard, and in the sense that they subsist 'outside time' (and, presumably, 'outside space' as well). And in this way the subject-matter of history is made to appear very mysterious indeed, demanding tentative handling and esoteric methods. We may well ask, under these conditions, how it is possible to 'know someone else's activity of thinking'. Yet the theory was constructed primarily in order to explain this process.

What seems to have happened here is an occurrence not infrequent in philosophy. A proposition is thought to be in need of explanation: the explanation provided by the philosopher turns out to be a restatement of the original *explicandum*, but formulated in different, more figurative language. In place of the statement, 'people think of the same idea, or come to the same conclusion, at different times', we are told that objects and acts of thought stand outside time, that they endure through time, and are capable of being revived at intervals; and this is merely a complicated, Heath Robinson way of saying the same thing (although its phrasing is a great deal more misleading).

Leaving until later a fuller discussion, the following is immediately relevant:

1. History is primarily concerned with human beings and what they have done. When the historian comes to ask why they did what they did, he sometimes answers by referring to general laws of human response to specified types of situation; and sometimes by referring to what Professor Popper has called 'the logic of the situation', i.e. in terms of what it would be reasonable to do in such-and-such circumstances, and with such-and-such objectives in view. To say 'all history is the history of thought' is to recommend, presumably, that all historical explanation should be of the latter type. This recipe is not particularly convenient, since all human activity is not 'thought out'—it may be routine, skilled, or impulsive, for example: further, the behaviour of human beings *en masse* rather than *qua* individuals is not easily covered by it.

2. The first type of explanation mentioned in (1) may broadly be called explanation in terms of 'causes' and 'effects'; the second type, explanation in terms of 'intentions' and 'plans'.

Now—and this is important—in *both* instances we are explaining what human beings have done in particular situations. This is worthy of emphasis because it draws attention to the fact that the actual practice of historians does not bear out the theory that the subject-matter of history is distinct from the subject-matter of other branches of inquiry in such a way as to render the categories used in the latter inappropriate to it. While (as has been pointed out) it is true that it makes nonsense to speak of 'inanimate matter' being motivated, having intentions, and so on, and while it is true that actions of human beings are frequently accounted for in this way, it does not thereby follow that we cannot generalize about human behaviour or that 'animate matter' is not amenable to scientific treatment. 'He let out a cry because he stubbed his toe' is an explanation in virtue of a generalization about how people behave when they stub their toes.[1] Nor is there any conflict or incompatibility between explanations of this kind, and explanations in terms of thoughts and intentions. We can explain a man's action upon being threatened by a black-mailer both in terms of a generalization about how people react when their interests are threatened, and in terms of a specific plan which the man evolved in order to meet the danger, e.g. 'he went to the police because he decided it was the best thing to do in the circumstances'. There is no *clash* between the two: which we choose depends upon our interest and purposes. The beliefs that there must be such a clash, or that causal explanation is extrinsic to history, have their origin in the model of the historian as a man who treats exclusively of mental events and processes which are set behind the physical actions of human beings, pulling the strings, as it

---

[1] The part played by generalizations about human nature in all branches of activity is well stated by Hume. See *Treatise of Human Nature*, vol. ii, pp. 116 ff. (Everyman Edition).

were. 'Thoughts' and 'plans' are not substitutes for 'causes' which operate on a different sphere of existence; that is why it is muddling to say, for instance, that 'cause' for an historian 'means the thought in the mind of the agent', suggesting an invisible engine or microbe. The two forms of explanation are different and it is a mistake to try to conflate them.

Thus, in conclusion, I would say that there is truth in the assertion that the subject-matter of history involves the use of categories of explanation apart from those that have reference to causal laws, if by this it is merely meant that we *can* account for human behaviour in non-causal terms. But I would reject the views (*a*) that human behaviour can be correctly interpreted *only* in non-causal terms (*b*) that in history we have to do with a world of 'mental agencies', mysteriously lying behind the world of physical bodies and actions, separate from it and yet controlling it.

§ 5. *The Language of Historical Description*

I T is frequently asserted that the subject-matter of history has an irreducible vagueness and complexity, an essential 'thickness', which makes all attempts to regard historical work as in any way comparable to natural science futile, or, at best, inconclusive. In history we seem to be presented with huge chunks of fact that obstinately refuse to fit into the tidy compartments of a scientific system. The subject-matter of history spills over, and swamps us in its variety and its richness; confuses us with its queer habit of being highly general and minutely particular at one and the same time. If history is not bunk, it is at least a mess, or a 'series of messes', as E. M. Forster once described it. And we remember what H. A. L. Fisher wrote in his *History of Europe* (vol. i, p. vii): 'I can see only one emergency following upon another as wave follows wave, only one great fact with respect to which, since it is unique, there can be no generalizations.'[1]

---

[1] See also K. R. Popper, *The Open Society and Its Enemies*, vol. ii, p. 185. Popper writes: 'Indeed it is necessary to recognize . . . that everything is possible in human affairs.' It should be noted, however, that, in this context, Professor

While much of this is undeniable, it is misleadingly stated. For it suggests that there is something 'wrong' with history for being as it is, and that, if only history were akin to science, we should be confronted by a more satisfactory state of affairs. It also suggests that it is what the historian is talking and writing about that causes the difficulty: it is the material of history that is intransigent. And, finally, are we indeed forced to accept Fisher's conclusion? I think not. Yet there is truth in what has been said. How is it to be accounted for?

In Part I the relationship between science and common-sense was briefly discussed. It was pointed out that the formation of certain concepts with a precise definition (e.g. a defining property of phosphorus is melting at 44° C.) was a characteristic of the development of any particular branch of science, and that one of the difficulties of some studies (e.g. sociology) was the looseness and awkwardness of the concepts or terms employed. The same 'trouble' occurs with history. Suppose, for instance, that an historian informs us that discontent amongst the peasantry always leads to revolution. The scientifically minded person is unlikely to be satisfied with this generalization for the simple reason that it is too indefinite, leaves too much unspecified. At what stage, he may ask the historian, does irritation and dissatisfaction amount to discontent? And how much discontent must there be to justify our expectations of the occurrence of a revolution? Are there different kinds of discontent, and, if so, what kind is required by the generalization? Is there a method of measuring discontent? Can we, for example, conclude with certainty that when such-and-such a percentage of the peasantry are discontented to such-and-such a degree the expected revolution will take place? Is there a time-interval which can be specified? And what about the revolution itself? Can we predict from the degree of discontent the precise intensity and duration of the revolution? How is the intensity

Popper is arguing against certain formulations of historical determinism, viz. those of Marx, Hegel, and Comte. See also his 'Poverty of Historicism', *Economica*, 1944–5.

of a revolution measured? The series of possible questions is infinite.

The historian will hedge and protest in the face of this barrage. He will submit that he did not intend his 'remark' (a word incidentally foreign to scientific discourse) about revolutions to be interpreted as strictly as this, or that it is not his job to give rules for the prediction of future historical developments. At the back of his mind will lurk the suspicion that somehow these are improper questions. And he will be right. There is something fishy about asking the historian questions of a type we should feel justified in asking a theoretical or practical scientist. How is this to be explained?

The answer brings to light an important feature of historical writing which inclines us against calling it a science. As has been pointed out, the language in which the discoveries of any particular branch of scientific inquiry are expressed is adapted to the systematically organized body of laws or hypotheses which constitutes that branch of inquiry. Consequently the concepts employed by a particular science have a more or less precise definition. For example, when the scientist discusses phosphorus, we know that he has in mind a certain measurable criterion according to which it is possible to decide whether a given substance is phosphorus or whether it is not. Scientific concepts are introduced when a particular empirical correlation has become analytic within the scientific system in question: such concepts are useful in order conveniently to refer to an indefinite number of observed correlations of a certain type. They are shorthand devices. Berkeley showed this long ago, when, writing about gravitation, he said:

But a philosopher, whose thoughts take in a larger compass of nature [than those of most men], having observed a certain similitude of appearances as well in the heavens as the earth, that argue innumerable bodies to have a mutual tendency towards each other, which he denotes by the general name attraction, whatever can be reduced to that he thinks justly accounted for.

And again, in the next section, we find him saying:

If therefore we consider the difference there is betwixt natural philosophers (i.e. scientists) and other men, with regard to their knowledge of the phaenomena, we shall find it consists, not in an exacter knowledge of the efficient cause that produces them . . . but only in a greater largeness of comprehension, whereby analogies, harmonies and agreements are discovered in the works of nature, and the particular effects explained, i.e. reduced to general rules . . .[1]

In historical writing, on the other hand, the reference to a system of interrelated and interdependent statements, embodying precise correlations between selected features of experience, is lacking; and in consequence we find also absent the usage of concepts whose meanings can be expressed in exact terms. While there exist definite and recognized procedures according to which sentences that contain the word 'gravitation' may be transformed into other sentences containing references to statements of measurable correlation, we are on different ground when we approach sentences containing words like 'revolution' or 'feudalism'. For the logic, the behaviour, of these words is not the same. This is brought out if someone says: 'The intensity of a revolution varies proportionately to the degree of peasant discontent which preceded it.' For how are we supposed to be able to settle the validity of such an assertion?

It is at this point that people are liable to complain that there is something 'wrong' with history. If 'wrong' is persuasively defined to mean 'lacking the structure of a developed science' then we must agree that there is something wrong with it. But why should history possess such a structure? We have seen already that the historian is not *interested* in formulating general hypotheses or in making predictions; he is interested principally in finding out what happened and in describing what happened in all its detail: and it follows from this that he is interested in talking about a great many varying aspects of past human experience and activity at once. He is hence not primarily concerned with the isolation of certain features of his material, nor with the extensive universalization and abstraction that we associate with science. It is, of

[1] *Principles of Human Knowledge*, sections 104 and 105.

course, open to anybody to say that history should strive to become more scientific, that it should seek more precise correlations within its material than those with which it has been satisfied up to now, that it should reformulate its concepts. This may or may not be an attainable goal. But, when making such recommendations, we must beware of prescribing that history should become other than it is: for then, like Alice in Wonderland, we may find that the baby in our arms has turned into a pig.

Thus there is a fundamental distinction between the languages respectively used by the historian and the scientist to describe the characteristics of the world in which they are interested. I want now to consider some of the consequences of this distinction, and first to·show how a misunderstanding, or a dimly grasped understanding, of its existence may lead to the formulation of unwarrantable conclusions regarding the subject-matter of history. And it is, paradoxically enough, at root the same misconception which leads some philosophers (and some historians as well, when they have come to talk about their subject) to say that history can, and ought to be, made scientific, and which leads others to say, not only that it can never be made scientific, but, further, that historical procedure is utterly unrelated to scientific procedure and that the two must be kept rigidly apart.

The root misconception is, I suggest, the theory of meaning which maintains that language mirrors, copies, or pictures reality. The meaning of every word is an object, and every sentence is in some sense or other a reflection of a state of affairs or a fact. Some sentences (hypotheticals, negative sentences) cause trouble, and recondite facts have to be found, or postulated, for them to reflect. To change the metaphor, houses have to be constructed for these 'homeless entities'.[1]

This is not the place to argue about how words and sentences mean. I shall merely dogmatically assert that the 'snapshot' theory of language is mistaken, and that language is more

[1] See I. Berlin, 'Logical Translation', *Proceedings of the Aristotelian Society*, 1949–50.

profitably viewed when the wide variety of functions it may perform has been appreciated. And then, as was seen earlier when the relationship between common sense and science was discussed, it becomes clearer that the kind of language we use is related to our purposes and interests, to what we are trying to do and the situation in which at any time we find ourselves. We no more always want to talk science than we always want to talk common sense.

The theory of 'logical constructions' at least taught the need for care when discussing words like 'revolution', or 'state' or 'civilization': it was most successful when there was no 'sense-datum' axe to grind. And while it is not necessarily misleading to say that history is concerned with societies, civilizations, nations, movements, and so forth, any more than it is misleading to say that physics is concerned with electrons, protons, and light-waves or psychology with the unconscious and repressed memories, provided all that is meant is that there is a *use* for those terms in history, physics, and psychology respectively, it is, on the other hand, extremely misleading if it is taken to mean that the historian is concerned with entities of a peculiar and *recherché* nature. For this would be equivalent to presenting a picture of the world where wars and revolutions lay side by side with atoms and electrons and tables and chairs; and it would thus put the distinction between the subject-matter of the scientist and the historian in a highly confusing manner. Just as carpenters and builders attend to tables and houses respectively, so we should be inclined to say that physicists and historians attend to electrons and revolutions respectively. Yet it is this story that the 'mirror-fact' theory of language in its crudest form encourages, with the result that human beings and unconscious minds and revolutions are depicted as crowded one on top of the other in a kind of vast jumble sale, each waiting for the appropriate customer (whether he be psychologist, historian, or 'ordinary man') to buy it.[1]

---

[1] This fallacy was, I think, what Croce had in mind when, in his *Logic*, p. 304, he wrote of the failure to understand 'the introduction of empirical

It may be protested that this is, to say the least, an exaggeration, and that no one has seriously supposed that history and science could be distinguished in such a manner. I do not suggest, however, that it has ever been either held or stated in so bald a form. Yet a glance into the pages of Hegel,[1] Engels, or Spengler may be sufficient to arouse the suspicion that at any rate some view of the kind underlay much of what they wrote. Even an explicitly used metaphor may be dangerous, may outlast its temporary *ad hoc* function of providing a picturesque but not too serious analogy, and live on to colour the remainder of an author's work on a particular topic. One wonders whether Dr. Toynbee's comparison of vanished civilizations with 'fossils', and his talk of 'dead' and 'living' civilizations, may not have influenced him more than he has perhaps been aware.[2] And likewise we may experience uneasiness when Marxians speak of the 'substructure and superstructure' of societies, and of 'economic forces necessitating change'.

If this theory of the subject-matter of history is taken into account it is easy to see how certain features of the science

concepts' whose function is 'to divide the mass of historical facts and to regroup them conveniently for mnemonic purposes'. 'We should not be deceived by finding them fused in historical works (which continually have recourse to such aids to memory) nor allow ourselves to forget that their function is *subservient*, not *constitutive*.'

[1] In *The Philosophy of History*, Introduction, p. 53, Hegel writes: 'Each particular National Genius is to be treated as only One Individual in the process of Universal History.'

[2] It is only fair to Toynbee to point out that, after quoting a passage from G. D. H. Cole's *Social Theory* which attacks attempts to identify societies with mechanisms, organisms, &c., he explicitly asserts that 'human society is a system of relationships between human beings who are not only individuals but are also social animals in the sense that they do not exist at all without being in this relationship to one another' (*Study of History*, vol. i). Elsewhere, in his book *Civilisation on Trial*, Toynbee gives this definition of what he means by 'civilization': 'I mean . . . the smallest unit of historical study at which one arrives when one tries to understand the history of one's own country.' According to this interpretation, the term 'civilization' appears to be treated as a 'methodological concept'. Toynbee is, in effect, saying: 'Study history in terms of civilizations', i.e., he is prescribing a method of doing history which entails, among other things, treating the history of individual states in terms of their relations with other states, and in terms of the leading political ideas, traditions, and scientific techniques common to these states. And here the only question that can legitimately be asked is whether this method is fruitful or not.

versus history controversy have been affected by it. We have before us the view that certain entities—civilizations, states, and so forth—are the sacred preserve of the historian. And the question is then put: what is to be done with them? Are they amenable to ordinary inductive treatment, i.e. can they be generalized about? Or, on the contrary, is this impossible? And, if the reply to this is in the affirmative, can some other method be found for making predictions about them?

One answer to these questions states boldly that the subject-matter of history is amenable to ordinary inductive treatment. History admittedly differs from science in that it has to do with different objects; nevertheless these objects can be generalized about, the behaviour of one such object can be correlated with the behaviour of another such object. And, if sufficient generalizations are made on a wide enough scale, why should not the body of such generalizations be called a science? Historians have been doing the spade-work for such a science for hundreds of years: now all that is necessary is to gather together the information they have collected and throw it into the form of laws.

The stock objection to this is that it is easier said than done. It is felt, as was said at the beginning of this section, that the 'things' or events with which history deals are too big and unwieldy, too complex and various, to be generalized about. They overflow the edges of any precise classification. We are asked to compare the English Revolution of the seventeenth century, the French Revolution, and the Russian Revolution, and to recognize their dissimilarities with one another, the futility of attempting to put them all into one basket.

Consequently, an alternative view is presented. According to this, we are asked to accept the diversity between the subject-matter of history and 'the sciences', and to realize that the nature of history will not permit of the formulation of laws in the scientific sense of the term, namely, by means of correlations observed to hold in experience. Nevertheless, it is possible to grasp the meaning of an historical entity like a civilization, to 'understand' it, by means of historical insight, which represents the faculty of the historian for penetrating into the essence of the objects of his study, and for coming to know the 'principle of development' of a nation, social movement, or class.

The claim that we are bound to choose between these two alternative interpretations is, however, unwarranted. Historical generalizations have not the status of scientific laws, but this does not mean that we must deny their existence altogether and look for a different method of understanding history. Nor is it the case that in history we suddenly find ourselves faced with peculiar intractable entities that refuse to be 'fitted in'. The difficulty in question is a reflection of the language of historical description, and once this is recognized it is seen no longer to be a difficulty but an entirely natural outcome of the usage of this language.

Thus the stock objection to the first alternative is right (in a sense) to stress the fact that revolutions, for example, cannot tidily be correlated, one with another, but it is wrong or misleading to put this down to a recalcitrance inherent in the nature of the material of history. The latter supposition originates in a mistaken view of the historian's subject-matter. Historians write about what people have done, felt, said, and so on. And this does not mean that it is not possible also to write scientifically about what people have done, felt, and said. Psychologists and physiologists, for example, have a considerable interest in various aspects of human behaviour. But their description takes a different form. And this difference in form is a reflection of differences in purpose and interest, and consequently of method. Nor is this strange: naturalists and honey-vendors are both concerned with bees, but this does not mean that they will not handle them in different ways. As a result we find historians and scientists often discussing the same occurrence in very different fashions: it is only necessary to imagine the variations we should discover in the respective reports of an historian and a geologist concerning the eruption of Vesuvius in A.D. 79 or in the respective reports of an historian and a psychologist on the mental condition of Alexander I of Russia during his last years to appreciate this.

Language used for certain purposes requires a conceptual apparatus different from that required by language used for other purposes. Historical concepts like 'revolution' were not evolved to meet the descriptive needs of an expanding scientific system; they were developed to meet the requirements of those who wanted a short means of referring to a fairly common instance of the behaviour of human beings in society. The historian is concerned with human activities, and he is principally interested in those activities in so far as they have been found related to one another in social groups; to speak conveniently about the multitude of interrelated activities with which he finds himself confronted he uses short-hand terms like 'revolution'. When asked what such terms mean he points to less complicated events, like mob-riots, changes in government, and so forth, and says that it is to the occurrence of events of this type that he refers when he says that a revolution has happened. What he does not do is to lay it down explicitly that any single event or set of events must be present if a social movement is to be called a revolution. He does not, to take a fantastic example, make it a necessary truth-condition of the statement 'a revolution has occurred' that at least 40 per cent. of the total male population should have appeared armed in the streets, shouting subversive slogans. To restrict the use of the term in this manner would be equivalent to eliminating its utility as a means of referring to a large number of social movements of varying types occurring at different times. And this is precisely what he wishes it to be able to do.

The crux of the distinction between the historian and the scientist is as follows. The scientist frames hypotheses of precision and wide generality by a continual refining away of irrelevant factors. Things are otherwise with the historian. His aim is to talk about what happened on particular occasions in all its variety, all its richness, and his terminology is adapted to this object. That is the reason why terms like 'revolution' are left so vague and so open. They are accommodating terms, able to cover a vast number of events falling within an indefinitely circumscribed range. His concepts have spread: but this spread involves a complementary limitation, a limitation upon the generalizations in which they may occur. Generalizations about revolutions, class-struggles, civilizations, must *inevitably* be vague, open to a multitude of exceptions and saving clauses, because of the looseness of the terms they employ. As it has been said, '. . . on tâchera de préciser les termes du rapport, de telle sorte que tous les cas particuliers répondent exactement au concept. Mais, à mesure que l'on se rapproche ainsi du concret, on élimine la généralité'.[1] But this is not to criticize such generalizations provided that they are not expected to do more work than they are fitted for. The scientific model of precise correlation is misleading in any attempt to comprehend the role of these generalizations in history, where they function frequently as *guides to understanding*.

To conclude, we may, if we choose, say that the subject-matter of history is different from that of science. But we must be careful. We must not take this to mean that the historian is dealing with queer entities, lying about the world or salvaged from the deep-sea forests of the past. The world is one: the ways we use to talk about it, various. And the fact that in some cases we decide to describe it in one way rather than another is contingent upon our purposes.

People are surprised that history cannot be turned into a science overnight. To explain this away, they suggest that there is something inherent in the nature of historical events themselves that makes this impossible. But we must question this. We must ask, first, whether it is ever justifiable to lay it down *a priori* that some feature of our experience is or is not capable of being subsumed under a general law. It is always possible to look for regularities, whether we are dealing with the behaviour of 'dead matter' or with the behaviour of living human beings. If we do not find regularities holding in the type of events we are examining, then we are at liberty to

[1] Raymond Aron, *Introduction à la Philosophie de l'Histoire*, p. 206.

signalize our failure by saying that the events in question are 'lawless'. But such a statement is merely a record of past failure. Secondly, we must ask what is meant by 'historical events'. If we are being told that people never act as we should expect them to act and that we cannot generalize about human behaviour, then the evidence of psychology in addition to that of the whole body of our common experience must be pointed to as a demonstration that what is being maintained is false, and, furthermore, that if it were true, ordinary day-to-day life as well as the study of history would be impossible. If, on the other hand, the complaint is that revolutions, wars, and civilizations cannot be neatly correlated, we must answer that there is here no reason for wonder or despair, but only a simple consequence of the purposes of the historian and of the language he uses to carry them out.

There are two further points I wish to make before concluding this section. The first concerns Fisher's statement, quoted at the beginning, that history represents 'one great fact with respect to which, since it is unique, there can be no generalizations'. This, however, may lead to a misunderstanding. There can, of course, be no generalization about the whole of history from the appearance of man on the planet to the present day, viewed as a single process: that is to assert a tautology, since generalization entails the existence of more than one event. In a like manner it might be argued that generalization about the universe is impossible, on the ground that we are only acquainted with one universe, not two or three or a hundred. But no one therefore assumes that science is impossible. And this is so for the very good reason that we do not attempt to generalize about the universe *as a whole*: scientists generalize about selected features occurring within it. Similarly, historians are at liberty to generalize about selected features of those events which make up the historical process. The obscurity of Fisher's statement rests upon the ambiguity of the phrase 'fact with respect to which'.

The second point concerns an article entitled 'Historical Explanation', by Mr. M. G. White, which appeared in *Mind*,

1943. Mr. White asks the question: What is the difference between an historical explanation and an explanation occurring in one of the sciences, e.g. biology? He points out that the characteristic of a biological explanation is the occurrence of specifically biological terms 'in an essential way'; and seems to consider that it must therefore be the characteristic of an historical explanation that there should occur within it specifically historical terms. This is surely false: at one point in his *English Social History*[1] Professor Trevelyan writes of the establishment of the 154 new hospitals and dispensaries in the 125 years after 1700, 'they were the outcome of individual initiative and of co-ordinated voluntary effort and subscription'. That is a bona fide historical explanation, but I can find no 'specifically historical terms' present. And the search for such terms appears to originate in the attempt to assimilate history to science in the manner which I have tried to show in this section to be pointless. It would be wearisome to repeat the thesis that specific scientific terminologies are a function of particular scientific systems, and that history presents us with no such system. There are, it is true, certain terms like 'revolution', 'class-struggle', and so forth which appear to be more historical than others, in the sense that they are found in history books more than elsewhere. But they are certainly not the preserve of history: journalists, propagandists, social reformers, politicians, novelists, even 'plain men', use them easily and with perfect propriety. The language in which history is written is for the most part the language of ordinary speech. And in this sense the comparison that has been drawn above between history and science may be said to resemble the comparison that was drawn in Part I between common sense and science, although it will later be seen that there are certain differences.

The upshot of what has been said regarding the subject-matter of history may be summarized as follows:

1. The pastness of historical events need occasion no problems of a metaphysical nature. Knowing that such-and-

[1] p. 345.

such an event occurred does not entail being 'directly acquainted' with the event in question: it does entail, however, being able to produce evidence for its past existence. It is, of course, true that historical events are not repeatable under laboratory conditions and in this sense it may be argued that their being past presents a certain problem for historical explanation. To this point we shall return.

2. The fact that the historian's interest is directed upon particular events rather than upon universal laws is a fact about the purpose of history and not a fact about the type of event with which history deals.

3. The point that history deals with human actions under the aspect of their being planned, reasonable under the circumstances, &c., is the strongest argument that has been adduced to support the view that historical subject-matter is *sui generis*, in so far as it draws attention to the evident impropriety of attempting to interpret all the sentences of historians which include the word 'because' in terms of sentences containing reference to causal laws.

4. The contention that the subject-matter of history is *sui generis* on the grounds that history is concerned with special entities referred to by such words as 'revolution' and 'nation' is a mistaken notion based upon a misunderstanding of the function of historical concepts.

In what has been said, I have tried to indicate that a recognition of the differentia of historical writing as opposed to science does not commit us to an *a priori* position regarding the peculiarity of the subject-matter of history or regarding the impossibility or impropriety of using cause-and-effect as a legitimate category of historical explanation. The way in which this category functions in history must now be considered.

PART III

CAUSAL CONNEXION IN HISTORY

§ 1. *How do Historians Explain?*

IN the previous two parts of this book we have taken as our starting-point the regularity interpretation of explanation and have devoted a considerable amount of space to examining arguments which purport to show that an extension of this interpretation into the domain of history is impossible. We have pointed out why the qualms experienced by upholders of such arguments are for the most part without foundation, although it has not been denied that they have succeeded in bringing to the fore distinctive features of historical writing too often forgotten by philosophers who have been over-impressed by the methodology of the advanced sciences. The task that now confronts us is to consider the procedure historians in fact adopt to explain the events of which they treat; and it will be argued that their procedure as a whole is intelligible on the above interpretation, provided that the important differentiating characteristics of historical explanation are recognized, and provided that we make certain distinctions. For, as we have seen, there are explanations occurring in the work of historians that do not appear to square with the regularity interpretation in the manner discussed. There are also peculiarities in the routes used by historians to arrive at some of their explanations, and these peculiarities have had, it will later be contended, a powerful influence upon the treatment of the subject by many philosophers.

The kinds of difficulties that will confront us may be illustrated by giving a list of some examples taken from history-books.

1. 'Louis XIV died unpopular . . . having caused France to lose . . . the incomparable position she had gained by the policy of the cardinals.'[1]

[1] Charles Seignobos, *A History of the French People*, p. 261.

2. 'The conditions were favourable to a revolution. The government had no military forces at hand. The working-class was passing through an acute stage of unemployment . . .'[1]

3. 'A generation of acute rebels was being prepared, because the lack of every liberty, which hinders the formation of a culture that implies discernment and criticism, turned the minds of students either to turbid daydreams . . . or to abstract and simplifying rationalism . . .'[2]

4. 'Patronage was the root cause of a long series of secessions of Presbyterian bodies from an Established Church bound by this State-made law.'[3]

5. 'The great improvement in professional skill was supported by the foundation of hospitals . . .'[4]

6. 'As an event in human history, the [Great] War was caused by human psychology.'[5]

7. 'It is the relation of social forces which, in the last analysis, explains the fact that Louis XV's character, and the caprices of his favourite, could have such a deplorable influence on the fate of France.'[6]

8. 'Oddly enough, when he came to the revolt he emphasized first his own personal wrongs . . . in order to show that he had fought only for what was his own. This again was sound feudal theory.'[7]

9. 'After setting Talleyrand aside from the conduct of affairs he had brought him back. Why? Because the Emperor, always inclined to be variable when he felt secure in the saddle, required for this task of diplomatic consolidation a subtle and tactful man . . .'[8]

10. 'Despising the enemy, the author of the New Model made preparations worthy of Buckingham.'[9]

11. 'To one holding such a creed economic individualism was hardly less abhorrent than religious non-conformity, and its repression was a not less obvious duty. . . . It is natural therefore that Laud's utterances and activities in the matter of social policy should

[1] Charles Seignobos, *A History of the French People*, p. 285.
[2] Benedetto Croce, *A History of Europe in the Nineteenth Century*, p. 188.
[3] G. M. Trevelyan, *English Social History*, p. 461.
[4] Ibid., p. 345.
[5] Leonard Woolf, *After the Deluge*, p. 27.
[6] G. Plekhanov, *The Rôle of the Individual in History*, p. 34. Pamphlet published in English by the Foreign Languages Publishing House, Moscow, 1946.
[7] C. V. Wedgwood, *William the Silent*, p. 220.
[8] Jacques Bainville, *Napoleon*, p. 276.
[9] Trevelyan, *England under the Tudors and Stuarts*, p. 323.

have shown a strong bias in favour of the control of economic relations by an authoritarian State . . .'[1]

12. 'The classic tradition was shattered, because Islam had destroyed the ancient unity of the Mediterranean.'[2]

13. 'The general significance [of the age of Mercian supremacy] is plain. . . . With all its weaknesses the system marks the first advance ever made on a great scale towards the political unity of England.'[3]

A proportion of these examples—roughly (1)–(7)—fit fairly easily into the regularity pattern, some kind of general statement is implied by their assertion. They appear to be of the same form as the statements: 'The window broke because a stone hit it' or 'The billiard-ball moved because another billiard-ball collided with it', where the speaker, when asserting the occurrence of two events, uses a general hypothetical statement to relate the two occurrences one to the other. This is made particularly clear in (2), for example, where the historian refers to working-class discontent and government weakness as conditions likely to promote the outbreak of a revolution, and in (3) where a general law concerning intellectual development under despotic rule is explicitly stated. About (6) we may feel doubtful, although our doubts here are a consequence of the apparent pointlessness[4] of the explanation provided rather than of its structure. Again, examples which contain reference to a 'root cause' or to factors which 'in the last analysis' determine a particular historical phenomenon, while they undoubtedly require careful analysis, would not seem to be fundamentally different.[5]

On the other hand, the examples following (7) present problems. In these, the explanation involved would not naturally be called 'causal': in some we should speak more naturally of 'motives', 'intentions', 'attitudes', or 'reasons'. (12) might be interpreted as illustrating a feature of the historian's use of the expression 'the classic tradition'. And in (13) explanation seems

[1] R. H. Tawney, *Religion and the Rise of Capitalism*, p. 160.
[2] Henri Pirenne, *Mohammed and Charlemagne*, p. 185.
[3] F. M. Stenton, *Anglo-Saxon England*, p. 234.
[4] Perhaps due to isolation from its context.
[5] But see below, § 4.

to occur in a different sense again, the sense in which a development is shown to form an element in a pattern or trend.

Differences of this kind raise a point concerning the terminology of history. On stylistic grounds, or for reasons of economy, convenience, and so forth, the historian may make singularly little use of explanatory signposts like 'because', 'since', 'on account of', 'for the reason that', and so forth. A look through any history book shows the comparative rarity of the occurrence of these terms. Instead we find expressions like 'under the circumstances, it is not surprising that . . .', 'naturally at this point he . . .', 'it was inevitable that . . .', nouns like 'influence', 'motive-force', 'impulse', 'development', 'consequence', and verbs like 'lead to', 'result in', 'make', 'bring about', 'stimulate'.

The use of such words and expressions might be thought to shed an additional 'flood of darkness' over an already confused topic. It may be felt that it would be very much easier for the logician or the philosopher if only historians would take the trouble to insert, say, a 'because' signpost whenever they were providing an explanation, since we should then know exactly where we stood.

It is, of course, true that often the terminology of the historian (like the terminology of everyday speech) introduces explanations only 'implicitly'—under cover, so to speak— with the result that the historian frequently appears to be merely narrating where in fact he is also explaining. For example, we come across historians writing: 'The growing benevolence of the age was moved to cope with the appalling infant mortality'[1] (which means more than 'people decided to deal with the appalling infant mortality' since it also, in a sense, explains the decision they made) and: 'Very many people of all classes at the time of Waterloo knew the Bible with a real familiarity which raised their imaginations above the level of an insipid vulgarity of mind'.[2] And it might be

---

[1] Trevelyan, *English Social History*, p. 345.
[2] Ibid., p. 481.

held that this feature of historical writing disguises the obvious fact that explanation, the 'seeing of connexions', runs through and through all history and gives rise to the view, implicit in much philosophical work on the subject, that explanation is a somewhat surprising aspect of historiography. Its neglect may also be responsible for the more recondite philosophical accounts of the (exceedingly important) distinction between history and 'mere chronicle'.

It might also be argued that the historian's terminology is misleading in a more dangerous way. For may not his use of concepts like 'inevitability', 'impossibility', and 'necessity' and of metaphorical verbs like 'lead to', 'force', 'compel', 'make', give the impression that history is the story of man as a poor, wriggling creature held in the grip of a cruel, irrational Fate? Are we not ensnared in this way into accepting a Hardy-like picture of human endeavour, a picture which compares men to flies and the gods to 'wanton boys' who 'kill us for their sport'?

These arguments may have some justification, but it is doubtful whether the proposed attempt to make the language of the historian 'aseptic' would not lead to even greater trouble. There is always in philosophy a temptation to over-simplify, to boil down the stew of language, until only a watery mixture remains, insipid and almost unrecognizable after the 'reductive' process has been carried through to its bitter conclusion.

A truer insight into historical explanation will, I suggest, be obtained by accepting rather than suspecting the richness of the historian's vocabulary, and by avoiding attempts to force it into a preconceived pattern. When, for example, the historian writes that Napoleon was *induced* or *persuaded* or *led* by certain considerations to act in such-and-such a way, we do not feel that anything particularly misleading or difficult has been said, nor do we believe that we should be greatly enlightened if an attempt were made to show that the historian is really asserting a causal proposition in the ordinary sense. For words like 'induce' or 'persuade', as used in this type of context, seem to derive their meaning from something other than a presupposed regularity. Conduct-explanations are, indeed, a complex affair; but no good purpose is served by trying to force the unwilling and recalcitrant propositions into moulds which they do not fit. Such attempts too often end up, for example, in the postulation of a 'mental' causation, presumed to lie behind the physical movements of human beings; and our knowledge of its operation, because one of the terms of the postulated causal relation is in principle unobservable, has to be made dependent upon a kind of metaphysical second-sight. Problems may thus arise from a blunting of the distinctions expressed in the historian's terminology, an intransigent demand for uniformity at any cost.

Nevertheless, whatever may be the correct analysis of these awkward expressions, in this part I wish to concentrate upon analysing those cases where it is fairly clear that some kind of regularity between observable events is implied or assumed, where, for instance, historians make statements beginning 'conditions favoured . . .', 'a contributory cause was . . .', 'the good effects were counterbalanced by . . .', 'it was impossible under the circumstances to . . .', and so forth. We must try to discover what in general are the criteria which govern the historian's usage of expressions like these, and under what conditions it is justifiable to say that an 'historical connexion' exists between two events or states of affairs. Before this is attempted, however, a common misconception must be examined.

§ 2. Taine's Maxim

IN an interesting chapter of his book *The Theory and History of Historiography* called 'Ideal Genesis and Dissolution of the "Philosophy of History"', Croce quotes (p. 65) Taine's maxim: 'Après la collection des faits, la recherche des causes.' Croce disapproves strongly of this dictum, although some of the reasons he gives for his disapproval are quaint. Thus he begins by saying that 'it is very well known what happens when one fact is linked to another as its cause, forming a chain of causes and effects: we thus inaugurate an infinite regression, and we never succeed in finding the cause or causes to which we can finally attach the chain that we have been so industriously putting together'. This is an odd objection: odd, first, because of the picture it presents of causes being linked to one another to form a vast chain stretching into the mists of past time, secondly, because of the application of the logical notion of an 'infinite regress' to such a picture, and, thirdly, because of the suggestion implied that there is something wrong with a causal explanation if a First Cause is not found. It is legitimate to wonder how anything could ever be explained if such a stipulation were to be imposed universally. Nevertheless, there is much else in what Croce has to say about Taine's maxim that is shrewd and to the point, although his conclusions do not seem to me to be, in the main, acceptable. And the maxim may serve as a useful point of departure: for it is a dictum commonly thought to underlie historical procedure, it sums up shortly the most crudely 'positivistic' interpretation of history, and its inadequacy has proved to be a springboard for theories of historical explanation which are, in their way, equally misleading.

Taine draws a peculiar picture of the historian's activity. He depicts him as one who looks for, and, fortunately, sometimes finds, entities called 'facts' which are scattered about the world and who, then, having collected his discoveries and pinned them down like butterflies, inspects them more closely through a microscope to see if he can observe the tenuous threads connecting some of them together. These threads are causal connexions.

The peculiarity is in effect twofold:

1. There is the suggestion that a fact is an entity we can immediately recognize as soon as we come across it, each fact being neatly labelled for our benefit.
2. There is the suggestion that a causal connexion is similar to an invisible string which ties facts to one another.

Croce rejects this account, but in so doing he, like many Idealist philosophers of history, appears to think that he has discredited the role of causation in history altogether. The situation is analogous to that of someone who, having upon one occasion encountered a wolf in sheep's clothing, refuses ever afterwards to believe in the existence of real sheep. For Croce writes: 'The fact historically thought has no cause and no end outside itself, but only in itself, coincident with its real qualities and with its qualitative reality.'[1] Now this statement, if taken at its face-value, implies that a remark like 'It is a fact that such-and-such occurred, but I don't know why it occurred', which might be made as easily in common life as in history, is self-contradictory. But is it not true to say that we know that many things occurred without its also being the case that we know why they occurred? And to make it a rule of historical discourse that the word 'fact' may only be used when we know why what we are talking about occurred, to legislate that 'knowing x to be a fact' entails 'knowing the causes of x', appears to be a recommendation of doubtful value. Its net effect would be to impose an intolerable restriction upon the historian's usage of the word 'fact'.

It will be objected that this is not what Croce has in mind, and that when he writes, for example, that a fact 'has no cause . . . outside itself but only in itself' he means that the notion of cause as ordinarily understood does not enter into historical explanation at all, and that the appearance of paradox is only maintained in so far as a certain interpretation of causality is insisted upon.[2] What Croce is in effect saying is that only in so far as the experience of doing a certain action has been relived by an historian can the action itself be termed an historical fact: and that the process of 'reliving' carries with it the only form of explanation history requires. Re-enacting what happened in one's own mind *is* seeing why it happened.

The truth or otherwise of this contention is not relevant at this point. What is of immediate interest is that it represents an attempt to escape from Taine's story of the relationship

---

[1] Op. cit., p. 76.

[2] Cf. Collingwood, *Idea of History*, p. 214. 'For history, the object to be discovered is not the mere event, but the thought expressed in it. To discover that thought is already to understand it.'

between facts and causes, for Croce has seen that this story is implausible. I want to show why I think it is implausible, and then go on to point out that its implausibility does not entail the view that ordinary cause–effect explanations are outside the scope of history.

Croce spends some time discussing the notion of 'brute and disconnected' facts, observing that the existence of these is a presupposition upon which 'the causal method claims to start', and asserting that this presupposition has not only 'not been proved' but that it *cannot* be proved.[1] And for this statement there may be some justification, although historians do, not infrequently, have a sense for the expression 'brute facts', as we shall see. But the notion of fact is ambiguous.

Let us consider how the word 'fact' is ordinarily used. We can say such things as the following:

1. 'Napoleon's invasion of Russia in 1812 was a fact.'
2. 'This historical account is true to the facts.'
3. 'He has discovered a new fact about the French Revolution.'
4. 'Are you sure about your facts?'
5. 'You are now in possession of all the facts of the case.'
6. 'So that is your interpretation of the facts!'

These sentences can be restated in ways that bring out the differences between them.

Thus (1) might be restated as: 'It is true that Napoleon invaded Russia in 1812'; or as: 'The statement "Napoleon invaded Russia in 1812" is true.' When we use 'fact' in this sense we are talking about what really happened. A similar technique could be applied to (2). (3) might mean that someone had come across a fresh piece of evidence—a document, for instance—likely to have an important bearing upon our knowledge of the French Revolution; or it might mean, to take an example, that the statement 'Louis XVI went to Varennes in 1791' has been found to be false; and in this case

---

[1] Op. cit., p. 73.

the falsehood of the previously accepted statement would represent the 'new fact'.

Frequently, however, 'facts' simply means 'evidence': (5), for instance, might be the statement of a judge to a jury whose job it is to decide what really happened after hearing all the evidence produced at a trial. Again (6) could be the indignant cry of the accused after he has been found guilty of murder. But (4) again is ambiguous: the question might refer to the nature of the evidence from which it may be inferred that something or other took place: on the other hand, it might refer to the truth of an account that has been given of what happened upon a particular occasion.

Such ambiguities are important. The manner in which 'facts' may sometimes be equivalent to evidence shows in part how the idea has grown up that facts are always like the 'clues' Sherlock Holmes was wont to discover—cigarette ash, bloodstains, a slipper in the wrong place. With this model before us, it is easy to have the impression that there are mysterious entities called 'facts' which we find lying about the world, and that the 'fact-stating propositions' of historians, among others, are like mirrors held up to the past in which the facts that reside there can see their own reflection.

But this is misleading, especially when we come to treat of the facts that occur in history. Facts for the historian are not entities 'out there', ready-made for him to pick up. Unfortunately, the language in which philosophers have been accustomed to speak of the relation between descriptive sentences and what they describe has done much to encourage the latter picture. Statements, we are told, are 'compared with' facts, which suggests an analogy with the connoisseur comparing two paintings or a doctor comparing two X-ray photographs. Carnap also makes the point that the notion of comparing statements with facts leads to an 'absolutistic' view of a reality which remains fixed 'independently of the language used for its description'.[1] The 'correspondence theory of

---

[1] See R. Carnap, 'Truth and Confirmation'. (Republished in *Readings in Philosophical Analysis*, ed. Feigl and Sellars.)

truth' is likewise misleading as an account of how sentences are related to the non-linguistic world. Impressed by the 'direct contact' which some 'good' sensation and material-object sentences seem to make with reality—'I have toothache', 'There is a dagger before me'—philosophers have suggested that *all* sentences should 'correspond to the facts' in this sort of way if they are to be termed 'true'. But difficulties arise immediately other types of statements, which are not 'good' in the sense described, are considered: to what facts do assertions like: '$2+2 = 4$', 'if Hannibal had marched on Rome he would have taken it', 'Caesar crossed the Rubicon', 'the planets move according to Kepler's laws of motion' correspond? And, in consequence, new facts—mathematical facts, hypothetical facts, past facts, and so forth—have to be postulated in order to meet the bill. But this unwelcome procedure can be avoided provided that it is recognized that the conditions under which it is appropriate to consider different statements 'true' or 'false' vary, that I do not, for example, believe that, in order to be justified in calling 'true' the statement 'Caesar crossed the Rubicon', I must be able to produce evidence of the kind I produce when I wish to justify the truth of the statement that there is a dagger in front of me. And the assertion that a statement is true in so far as it corresponds to a fact merely blurs distinctions like this without adding anything informative. Indeed, the question: 'What do all statements correspond to?' is an illicit general question, similar to: 'What do all sentences mean?' Both invite odd answers: 'propositions' in the case of the second, 'facts' in the case of the first.

It is, of course, unobjectionable for someone to say of a statement that he knows that it 'represents a fact'. For this is another way of saying that he has good reasons for considering his statement to be true, that he can produce conclusive evidence for it. But once again the phrase 'representing a fact' must not be misconstrued as being used as it is used in the statement: 'this pepper-pot represents the batsman and this salt-cellar the bowler' or in: 'Mr. *X* represents the Ministry of Agriculture.' People also tend to speak of statements 'fitting facts', rather as hats fit heads and keys fit locks.

What has been said also bears upon the meaning of the phrase 'so-and-so knows the facts' or 'is in possession of the facts'. For we do not know facts in the way that we know people, or possess them in the way that we possess motor-cars. And we do not collect them in the way that we collect stamps. 'Collecting evidence' may have this sense: 'collecting facts' has not—or only if it is used in the sense of 'collecting evidence' (see above).

It is, I think, such considerations as these that account for the strangeness of speaking of the historian as, first, collecting the facts and, secondly, looking for the causes. If by 'collecting facts' we mean the amassing of evidence, it is clearly incorrect to say that, after this operation has been carried out, the historian then goes on to investigate the causal relationships subsisting between the various objects which compose his evidence.

What, then, is meant by the expression 'collecting the facts'? Let us imagine that somebody wants to discover the facts about the French Revolution. How will he set about it? To start with he will probably get together and inspect all the documents, books, and so forth relevant to the subject. By doing so he will come to see what happened, acquire a knowledge of the period. In what does this process consist? I suggest that it consists, amongst other things, in learning, not merely that such-and-such event occurred at such-and-such a date, but, in addition to this, recognizing that there are relations between the events, recognizing, for example, that the calling of the Estates-General in 1789 was connected with the state of government finances at the time. Indeed, part of the grounds for believing that a given event occurred may consist in knowing of the existence of certain conditions which would 'favour' the occurrence of such an event. Evidence may lead the historian to infer that x occurred. Believing that x occurred may lead him to expect that as a result y occurred. And fresh evidence may come to light which confirms this hypothesis, or makes it more probable. And, in turn, the belief that *y* occurred may have a bearing upon the occurrence of some other event which had been accepted as having happened before, but which now, in the light of this new belief, may no longer be taken for granted.

This would seem to be a reasonable account of what in part is meant by 'finding out the facts' about an historical topic or period. And if it is, then there are certain features worthy of attention:

1. It does *not* entail a search for 'bare, brute, isolated facts'.
2. It does entail the examination of evidence in order to make, amplify, correct, or replace inferences to the occurrence of past events.

The latter procedure is not, of course, as simple as it appears. It is not a matter of finding a document stating that such-and-such a thing happened on such-and-such an occasion, and automatically inferring from this that the event described took place.

(*a*) Evidence is not always reliable. It must be compared with the evidence of other authorities and witnesses: it must be tested with reference to what knowledge we already possess of the period as a whole, and with reference to our experience of what can be expected to occur under certain types of circumstances: and it must be judged in the light of what we believe to have been the character and likely sentiments and purposes of the writer of the document we are considering. This latter point is important; for, if we know that the document is a lie or that it is intentionally misleading, we must ask *why* it is a lie or misleading; and this may provide us with fresh and perhaps fruitful hypotheses that can be tested against further evidence.[1]

(*b*) In assessing whether or not a certain past event occurred, the historian does not conceive of such an event as taking place in a vacuum. On the contrary, he regards it as occurring within the context of a network of other events related to it,

---

[1] See Collingwood's salutary attack upon 'scissors-and-paste' methodology, *Idea of History*, pp. 278 ff.; also his *Autobiography*.

and this assumed interconnexion is not only an important criterion for deciding about the reliability of specific inferences he may make from evidence at his disposal, but in addition it frequently leads him on to the postulation of other events which his evidence has so far not suggested, but which future investigation may confirm.

It should by now be possible to see why Taine's interpretation of historical method is so misleading. For his dictum suggests, amongst other things, that the finding out what happened and the finding out why it happened are two distinct procedures. And this is not the case. It is incorrect to speak of 'finding out the facts' as if it were a process separate from, and prior to, the discovery of causal relations: there is what may be called a *procedural interconnexion* between the two.

How did Taine's muddle arise?

There appear to be three principal reasons. The first is that Taine made the obvious confusion between facts and evidence. I say 'obvious' because it is clear at a glance that to say '*x* occurred' is not equivalent to saying 'There is evidence that *x* occurred': the ambiguity of the expression 'collection of the facts' may have led to his neglect of the distinction. Secondly, there is the puzzle over the word 'fact' itself. Croce writes: 'the mind thinks and constructs the fact'; and in so far as he means by this that facts are not entities in the sense pointed out above, that it makes nonsense, for example, to say that there is a fact in the next room while it is not nonsense to say that there is a table in the next room, he is surely right. (Unfortunately there has been a tendency to mix this truth up with the notion, discussed in Part II, that all historical facts are present facts.) Thirdly, to the belief that we discover facts in the way that we discover thimbles is added the suggestion that causes are threads linking facts together—a crusty fallacy that shares with old soldiers the distinction of never dying.

To conclude. While I believe that Croce was justified in his criticisms both of the dictum 'après la collection des faits, la recherche des causes' and of the view that facts are independent 'lumps', he was not justified in inferring from this that history has no use for causality. The procedure the historian uses to 'find out what happened' intimately involves what is implied by this concept. The mistake is only to suppose that there are two processes involved, one concerned with finding the facts, and the other with revealing the causal relations between them. What has been called the 'procedural inter-connexion' between fact-finding and 'seeing' causal relations should not, however, lead us to think that there is no difference between asserting a fact and asserting its explanation. Knowing that something is or was the case is different from learning, or getting to know, that something is or was the case. The way in which we achieve the latter may involve understanding why the event occurred, but it is surely incorrect to assume that our saying we know something or other to be an historical fact is equivalent to our saying we know precisely why it happened. The value of original historical work largely lies in bringing to light connexions between well-established historical facts, e.g. the revolutions of the year 1848, and other factors not previously recognized to be relevant. Marx's *Eighteenth Brumaire of Louis Bonaparte* is a case in point. Marx writes in his preface: 'I prove that the class-war in France created circumstances and relationships that enabled a gross mediocrity to strut about in a hero's garb', and his analysis seems to illuminate the historical event with which he is dealing, rendering certain features of it, that previously seemed strange, comprehensible. But in admitting this, we are not thereby justifying Taine. Marx did not begin by collecting facts, linking them together afterwards with 'causes'. His procedure was to start with an initial hypothesis which he used facts to confirm.

It should be emphasized that this account of the nature and discovery of historical facts does not entail any Idealist suggestion of their being 'mind-created' or 'subjective'—a suggestion by no means wholly absent from Croce's account. For we must respect the historian's insistence upon the objectivity of his inquiry and upon the necessity of neither distorting nor by-passing the facts. But taking facts into account in history is not like taking a road-block into account when driving a motor-car. There is no suggestion that if, in history, we do not respect them we shall, in some peculiar way, bump into them. This does not, however, entail that they are subjective or viciously mind-dependent. The matter appears to stand rather as follows. Historical statements, if they are to count as 'historical', must purport to describe what actually happened: this is a truism. It does not, of course, mean that what is thus represented may be seen or touched: the supposition that, since this is impossible, the historian's subject-matter must be 'in his mind' is, however, equally absurd.[1] Instead, we should recognize that there are historical statements which have attained a status so strongly supported by evidence, and which are so necessary to account for the occurrence of other historical events, that to deny them would be equivalent to making nonsense of large portions of history. We can imagine what would be the effect of denying the existence of the Roman Empire. And there are other statements that are sufficiently well attested to make the denial of their truth an unwarrantable, though less catastrophic, undertaking. Common to both is the dependence of 'the objectivity of historical facts' upon evidence. For, as often as not, to say that it is impossible to avoid the facts is equivalent to saying that it is impossible to ignore certain evidence, with the various implications such evidence may carry for a particular historical theory as to 'what really happened'. Professor Oakeshott is to be praised for insisting upon this point, however much we may wish to criticize some of the conclusions he has drawn from it.

§ 3. *The Problem of Historical Connexions*

IT was pointed out in the last section that the discovery of causal relations or connexions is not a feature of historical explanation only: it is also a feature of the discovery and establishment of historical facts. We must now consider what

---

[1] Cf. Croce's remark: 'True history is that of which an interior verification is possible' (op. cit., p. 136).

it is that historians are doing when they speak of two events as causally related to one another, and under what conditions it is deemed legitimate in history to say that two facts are connected.

This task is not made easier by the extreme vagueness of terms like 'connexion' and 'fact'.[1] We have already noticed a recalcitrance amongst some explanations when attempts are made to assimilate them to the ordinary causal pattern, and the connexion-between-facts terminology is apt to encourage the same confusions. Historians can say: 'Napoleon marched in order to invade Russia' but they can also say (at a pinch): 'The fact that Napoleon marched was connected with the fact that he intended to invade Russia.' There is also a wide variety of contexts in which the word 'connexion' may be used. Thus historians may say that there existed a connexion between Calvinism and the development of capitalism, or between the growth of liberal ideas in the nineteenth century and the contemporaneous rise of nationalist sentiment, or between the rise of Christianity and the Roman slave-system, or between the First World War and the competition for markets, or between the writings of Rousseau and the dictatorship of Robespierre, or between the German political tradition and the policies of Hitler. It would be rash to say that the connexions referred to in all these different contexts are of the same type, or that historians arrive at the decision that a connexion existed in precisely the same fashion for each of the cases considered. It is, indeed, blindness to this fact that partially explains many disputes that have arisen regarding the 'ultimate causal factor' in human affairs, including the well-worn conflict between materialist and idealist interpretations of history.

There is, however, a large number of cases where the connexion asserted by the historian causally relates one event, or set of events, to another event, or set of events, and it is with

---

[1] A vagueness which often makes it difficult to assess the precise point at issue in an historical controversy. See Tawney's criticisms of Weber in *Religion and the Rise of Capitalism* (note 32 to chapter iv and pp. 105–6).

these comparatively 'straightforward' cases that I wish here and in the subsequent section to deal. It is my aim to show that they may be analysed in terms of regularity, and that they share this in common with the commonsense and scientific types of explanation examined in Part I.

Nevertheless, there are considerable qualifications to be made. To begin with, our discussion of the subject-matter of history in Part II led us to recognize the dangers which beset anyone who blandly remarks that, after all, history is really a science; and to say that, if history is not science, then it must be common sense, is not satisfying, partially because 'common sense' is so vague a term.

Most commonsense explanations of a causal type are concerned with regularities of a comparatively simple kind—windows break when stones hit them, billiard-balls move when struck by other billiard-balls, trains dive to destruction when bridges collapse, people are hurt when their friends slander them. Such sequences occur time and again, and no one is surprised when a new instance is discovered.

Are historical explanations exactly like this? There is a temptation to say that they are not, and to resort to some such argument as the following.

In all causal explanations offered by historians two features are clear. First, certain individual facts are asserted as having taken place. In the first of the examples given in § 1 of this part, for instance, it was stated (1) that Louis XIV died unpopular, and (2) that he had pursued a policy of magnificence which had ruined France. Secondly, it is stated that a connexion existed between the two facts, and the recognition of this connexion is signified by means of the word 'because'.

So far so good. The historian tells a story. He is engaged upon describing what happened at a particular time and place and in what particular circumstances; and it is highly improbable that the precise concatenation of the various events and circumstances he describes will ever recur in that precise form. He is concerned with *that* war, *that* revolution, *that* per-

sonality, *that* death. He is not—a point too often forgotten—
primarily concerned with informing us what would or might
have happened if certain circumstances of the situation he is
describing had been different: nor is he concerned with
formulating for our further use 'historical laws' or formulae
by means of which we can predict what will happen in the
future when certain types of situation occur. As we have seen,
in this aspect his purpose is to be sharply distinguished from
that of the scientist—the biologist, physicist, or astronomer,
for example. History is the study of particular events: this
was what Croce was emphasizing when, in a passage previously quoted, he wrote: '. . . all the characteristics of History
can be reduced to the definition and identification of History
with the individual judgement', and what Bradley was
emphasizing when he said that the object of historical record
was 'the world of human individuality'.[1]

The historian also tells us why such-and-such an event took
place how and when it did. And it may be claimed that the
particularity of the connexion asserted by him is absolute:
that is to say, he is not treating of general correlations, in the
manner of science and even common sense; but of particular
connexions which may never again be repeated. The connexion between Louis XIV's policy and his death-bed unpopularity is an example. It is some such point as this that is
implied by the American philosopher, Maurice Mandelbaum,
when he writes:

> We have seen that history is differentiated from knowledge in the
> physical sciences in being a descriptive narration of a particular series
> of events which has taken place; in consisting not in the formulation of
> laws of which the particular case is an instance, but in the description
> of the *events in their actual determining relationships to each other*; in
> seeing events as the products and producers of change.[2] [Italics mine.]

This formulation of the notion of historical connexion is a
common one, but it is nevertheless mistaken. It is interesting

[1] F. H. Bradley, 'The Presuppositions of a Critical History', passim (*Selected Essays*, vol. i).
[2] M. Mandelbaum, *The Problem of Historical Knowledge*, pp. 13, 14.

that it should occur in the work referred to, because it shows
that even a philosophy of history written from an avowedly
empiricist standpoint can slip into the view that, when an
ᴴhistorian asserts the existence of a causal connexion between
two events, he can do so without reference to generalizations
of any kind: this is clearly indicated by Mandelbaum's explicit
exclusion of 'the formulation of laws of which the particular
case is an instance' from the sphere of historical explanation.
Mandelbaum's entire discussion of causality is indeed rendered
suspect by his refusal to recognize the nature of the relationship between causal connexions and laws or generalizations.
Thus he speaks of 'the fact that causal analysis is implicit in
scientific law, as well as being a presupposition of its formulation' (p. 237), of 'the formulation of scientific laws' depending
upon 'causal analysis' (p. 236), and of the fact that 'a scientific
law can always be retranslated into causal terms' (p. 237)—
whatever the last statement may mean. We read that 'before
such a reciprocal relationship (of the type found in Boyle's
law of gases) can be established, the scientist must determine
in specific cases that one event depends for its existence upon
another' (p. 237). Taken as a whole, the argument seems to
be that before a law or generalization can be established we
must first set about finding the *causal relationship* existing
between specific events: and we may then, and only then,
generalize these causal relationships into the form of a law.
And even when we obey this procedure, our laws will be
curiously inadequate: it will be the case that 'the causal
explanation of a particular instance may be quite different in
kind from anything into which a full-fledged scientific law
gives us insight. . . . A scientific law purports to hold of all
instances of a given "type". On the other hand, a full causal
explanation attempts to deal with the complete nature of our
instance. . . . Thus they [scientific laws] are not substitutes for
full causal explanations: their task is different in kind, and
their dependence upon causal analysis must not be allowed to
conceal this difference' (pp. 237–8).

The above account of the nature of causal relations is open

to criticism since it suggests that the discovery of a causal connexion and the formulation of a generalization or law are two
distinct processes, although the latter apparently 'presupposes',
or is founded upon, the former: the presumption seems to be
that a law is a generalization about previously detected causal
connexions. But if our knowledge of the existence of a causal
connexion is not dependent upon our having observed a
regularity in the concurrence of two events, we must ask in
what instead it can be said to consist. And here we are brought
back to the question forcibly put by Hume:

> Suppose two objects to be presented to us, of which the one is the
> cause and the other the effect; it is plain that from the simple considera-
> tion of one or both these objects, we never shall perceive the tie by
> which they are united, or be able certainly to pronounce, that there is a
> connexion between them. It is not, therefore, from any one instance
> that we arrive at the idea of cause and effect, of a necessary connexion
> of power, of force, of energy and of efficiency.[1]

Since elsewhere in his book Mandelbaum speaks with approval
of Hume, it is difficult to see how he could find this situation
other than embarrassing.

The trouble with the position adopted by Mandelbaum,
as with that adopted by so many other philosophers, lies in
his failure to recognize the extent to which causality is susceptible to further analysis, and in his consequent belief that
causal connexion is ultimate. Mandelbaum makes an heroic
effort to get the best of two worlds, but the net result is that
he treats the problem twice over. A law becomes a generalization about a number of specific causal connexions; but how
we come to know that a causal connexion holds in a particular
case remains a mystery.

It is not hard to disentangle the grounds for this muddle.
First, there is the misleading character of the 'stating-con-
nexions-between-facts' terminology, which has already been
criticized. A little more must be said about it, however. For
it gives the impression that the historian, when he uses the
term 'because' to connect the clauses of a statement, is affirming

[1] *Treatise of Human Nature*, p. 161.

the existence, not only of the two facts referred to in these clauses, but of an additional entity termed a 'connexion'. And it is easy to conclude that, since the two facts which are connected are individual facts, the connexion between them must be individual also. It is, of course, true that there is a difference between saying 'p and q' and saying 'p because q'; what would justify us in affirming the former would not justify us in affirming the latter. But the difference does not lie in the addition of an extra entity called a 'connexion'.

Secondly, there is the important point, true in history as well as in common life, that many causal connexions are 'intelligible' without an elaborate formulation of the generalization that is their warrant. When I am informed that my window is broken because a passer-by hurled a brick at it, I do not accept this explanation after performing a lengthy process of ratiocination about what happens on most occasions when bricks come into contact with window-panes. My familiarity with situations of this type is such that I have developed certain habitual responses to them.[1]

Thirdly, there is, in history, a tendency to regard all causal connexions as intelligible or 'intuitable' for another reason. For history treats of the actions of human beings, and we often *understand* the actions of other human beings on analogy with our own experience. And, although Mandelbaum in his book has little to say on this topic, it has perhaps unconsciously influenced his approach towards causal connexions in general. Understanding of this type certainly plays an important part in history, and cannot be ignored. Nevertheless, for the present I shall content myself with observing that it does not appear true to say that whenever an historian asserts the existence of a causal connexion between two historical events he does so on the analogy of what he would have done in the situation in question: the universal projection of his own character-traits upon persons living under totally different conditions, and of greatly varying background, temperament, and heredity would seem to be a risky business, quite apart

[1] Cf. Part I, § 3.

from the fact that it would lay him open to serious charges of subjectivity.[1]

The fourth and important reason for our present purposes lies in the fact that an event in history is frequently not so obviously a case of a given type as is an event treated by science or by common sense. A chemist may be able to tell us why a certain liquid behaved as it did on a particular occasion by referring to a law of the form 'Liquids of type H behave in such-and-such a way when heated to a temperature of such-and-such a degree Fahrenheit' and by pointing out that the liquid in question is of type H, that it was heated to the temperature specified and that it did behave in such a manner as to satisfy the requirements of the law. It is then possible (although not particularly happy since causal terminology suggests a temporal succession out of place in this context) to say that the heating of the liquid *caused* the unusual behaviour. Likewise, little worry of a philosophical nature is experienced when the man next door informs us that our windows are broken because he has spent the afternoon hurling bricks at them. We know about bricks and windows. But are we able to interpret with the same complacency the historian's explanation of the unpopularity of Louis XIV in terms of the generalization that rulers of nations become unpopular when they pursue a policy resulting in the decline of the country over which they rule? Does this rule always, or even usually, hold? And the difficulties increase when historians treat of more nebulous events like revolutions and wars and religious movements, when they depart from the concrete and consider more intangible entities. 'As a rough-and-ready generalization', it may be said, 'the view that wars have their origin in economic conflict is well enough but when we come to a particular war it is unsatisfactory. The historian wants to discover what were the causes of *this* war, and to achieve his aim he has to investigate his material in considerable detail. There are so many factors that may upset his generalization,

[1] There is, of course, the further difficulty that arises when the historian is dealing with mass-phenomena and not simply with individuals.

make it inapplicable.' And from this it is easy to return to the belief that the regularity interpretation of causality is out of place in history and that instead we must recognize that the historian looks for connexions 'subsisting in the real world' any one of which may be present on a unique occasion but may never occur again.

Are we obliged to accept this view, which makes nonsense of much that has so far been maintained? I think not. All the same, it is worthy of interest as an expression of the dissatisfaction that may be felt concerning the positivist account of historical explanation that is sometimes provided, the feeling that something has been left out. Professor Popper writes[1]

... we can never speak of cause and effect in an absolute way, but ... an event is a cause of another event ... relative to some universal law. However these universal laws are very often so trivial ... that as a rule we take them for granted, instead of making conscious use of them. ... If we explain, for example, the first division of Poland in 1772 by pointing out that it could not possibly resist the combined power of Russia, Prussia and Austria, then we are tacitly using some trivial universal law such as: 'If of two armies which are about equally well-armed and led, one has a tremendous superiority in men, then the other never wins.' Such a law might be described as a law of the sociology of military power; but it is too trivial ever to raise a serious problem for students of sociology, or to arouse their attention.

With Popper's statement that we cannot speak of cause and effect in an absolute way there is every reason to agree. He has also much of great interest to say (omitted from my quotation) of the 'infinite subject-matter' of history and of the necessity which this imposes upon the historian of choosing selective 'points of view' in order to organize his material.[2] In spite of this, however, there is a 'scientific' tone about his treatment of the problem that seems to me open to qualification on the grounds that, as it stands, it may suggest an artificial picture of what the historian is doing, an over-simplified, too tidy account. And the example he cites is perhaps too favourable to his own argument: the law is, as he says,

[1] *The Open Society and Its Enemies*, pp. 249 ff.
[2] The importance of these will be considered in the next section.

'trivial', but then so is the explanation—so trivial that probably few historians would bother to give it.

Let us return again to the explanation given as to why
Louis XIV died unpopular. The positivist interpretation
would be that Louis XIV represented a case of the law 'Rulers
are unpopular whenever their policies prove detrimental to
the fortunes of their countries' and that the explanation in
question was *deduced* from this law taken together with circumstances of the case. In this way it would be assimilated
to the explanation mentioned above of the behaviour of the
liquid which was heated to a definite degree of temperature.
But we can conceive of the historian objecting to this interpretation in the following terms: 'The assumption that the
case of Louis XIV is a case of a certain specified type is un-
convincing. Historians are not scientists, and the cases with
which they deal are not repeatable: there are no such things
as experiments in history. Nor are the generalizations they
use scientific laws; there are admittedly accurate tests that
can be performed to discover whether a liquid is of type H
or not and there are accurate tests for deciding its temperature
at a particular moment; in this way the scientist is enabled to
establish precise correlations, confirmable or falsifiable. The
statement that a liquid of type H behaved in manner b because
it was heated to a temperature t is a statement that, in one
sense, represents the confirmation of a particular scientific
law. But as an historian I would feel uneasy if it were suggested to me that my statement "Louis XIV was unpopular
because his policy was detrimental to France" represented a
confirmatory instance of an historical (or sociological) law of
the kind put forward. And this is not just because, as Popper
suggests, historians are not interested in establishing general
hypotheses. It is because I do not regard Louis XIV's unpopularity as being a case of any general hypothesis at all. I
regard it as the outcome of a particular complex of factors, a
complex which included Louis's expansionist foreign policy
and his wars, his heavy taxation, his court policy with its
disastrous effects upon the role of the nobility, his religious

persecution of the Huguenots and his attacks upon Jansenism. What in fact is historically important is to bring to light the nature of the connexion which existed between Louis XIV's policy and his unpopularity, and this is principally a matter of analysing in detail the particular case before me.'

If the above is representative of the kind of thing an historian might be expected to say, it is possible to recognize more clearly what is at issue, and also to see why there is a tendency to believe that historians treat of unique, never-to-be-repeated, connexions, that historical explanations are different in *kind* from scientific or commonsense explanations. The point may be brought out in a different way as follows.

When we have been given an explanation in chemistry of the type illustrated above, there is no more to be said: the explanation is complete. We can, if we choose, conduct further experiments to test the truth of the law that has been assumed, but there the matter ends. A similar belief that the explanation is relatively complete accompanies my hearing the next-door neighbour inform me that he has been throwing bricks at my windows. But now consider the case of the historical explanation. When an historian gives us an explanation of Louis XIV's unpopularity in terms of his policy, we want to know more about the form which Louis XIV's unpopularity took, more about the relationship between his unpopularity and those features of his policy that accounted for it, more about the relative weight and importance of those features in determining it. (It is significant, by the way, that Seignobos's explanation comes at the end of a chapter, as a summing-up of much that has already been said, as a concluding judgement upon the reign as a whole. This is an aspect of the part played by 'broad' historical explanations of this kind that is often overlooked; their role often consists in opening or in closing a discussion.)

A point relevant here has been made by Hempel in an article entitled 'The Function of General Laws in History'.[1]

[1] Carl Hempel, *Journal of Philosophy*, vol. 39, pp. 40 ff.

Hempel thinks that the reasons why philosophers have tended to believe that it is incorrect to speak of laws in history are two. First, it is tacitly taken for granted that we know on the whole how people behave. Secondly, there is 'the difficulty of formulating the underlying assumptions with sufficient precision and at the same time in such a way that they are in agreement with all the relevant empirical evidence available'. And he goes on to suggest that historical explanations are of the form of 'explanation sketches' which require 'filling out': that is to say, they require 'further empirical research'. Such an 'explanation sketch' 'points to directions where confirmation of the explanation may be found'. 'The filling-out process . . . will . . . assume the form of a gradually increasing precision of the formulations involved.'

It may be objected that the concept of an 'explanation sketch' is too vague. Let us try to make it more explicit.

In chemistry, if we are presented with a chemical of type H which behaves in a manner b, we can infer that it behaves as it does because it was heated to temperature t. And we are able to perform such an inference in virtue of a law which states the behaviour of chemicals of type H when heated to temperature t. And this law, which is used to explain the behaviour of the chemical on a particular occasion, is capable of direct confirmation or falsification by experiment. In history it is clear that the latter procedure is not possible. The historian cannot 'arrange' a revolution or a religious upheaval, or reproduce an economic crisis in a test-tube. And, in consequence, in the case of an asserted historical connexion, the historian cannot say: 'Since you do not believe what I say, let us try it out: let us vary the original conditions and see what happens.' But, it might be argued, can he not, even if experiment is impossible, even so observe similar cases that have occurred or are occurring? And can he not go on to say: 'In all cases where x has been ϕ or χ, x has been ψ, and in all cases where x has been neither ϕ nor χ, x has not been ψ. Therefore, in the particular case referred to, since x was not ϕ, it was ψ because it was χ?' In this way, it might be said, historical explanation may be satisfactorily assimilated to scientific explanation, and all will be well.

I think that the objection of anybody acquainted with historical procedure would be that it is not as simple as this. There is, of course, always a risk in moving from the general hypothetical or 'law' to the particular case, the risk that in the particular case factors unknown to us may have been present; but this is not a risk peculiar to history. The test-tube may be composed of peculiar glass;[1] again, the chemical may not be, as we thought, of type H but of type G. And it might, as a start, be said that the difficulty in history is simply that here the risk is very much greater than it is in most forms of scientific procedure. We frequently hear people (not only historians) speak of the 'imponderables' of history; and, when considering the course of future historical developments, the word 'speculate' is significantly used rather than the word 'predict'. Nevertheless, there is a further point of difference to be noted.

The historian may certainly believe that the generalization 'economic changes are accompanied by religious changes' has a *bearing* upon the problem of the Protestant Reformation in the sixteenth century. But he does not regard it as *applicable* in the way in which it might be true to say, for example, that the law of chemical change is applicable. In the case of the chemical law, the chemist knows where he stands. Definite procedures exist whereby it is possible to decide with a considerable degree of confidence whether, for example, the chemical is of a given type, and whether the experiment is conducted under 'normal' conditions; and in these circumstances the applicability or non-applicability of the law to the particular case is comparatively easy to determine. But the historian does not conform to this mode of procedure: his explanations are not 'read off' according to formulae, and, if it were suggested that they should be, he might object that history is not a science.

---

[1] See F. Waismann, 'Verifiability', *Proceedings of the Aristotelian Society* supplementary vol. xix, and G. H. von Wright, *The Logical Problem of Induction*, chap. iii, for discussions connected with the falsification of laws in science.

For, as was pointed out in an earlier section, history provides us with no system of precise correlations. Generalizations, in so far as they are enunciated by historians (and this is comparatively rare), are of an essentially loose and 'porous' nature. What was termed the 'spread' of the concepts that occur in their formulation allows of a considerable width of interpretation and permits a broad margin of exceptional cases. Historians do not expect their generalizations to be interpreted with any degree of strictness;[1] and when they are mentioned, they are introduced, if not apologetically, then at any rate with a considerable degree of reserve. They may be described as 'throwing light upon' a particular problem, as 'serving as a useful guiding thread', or as 'being relevant' to a question. They are spoken of as providing bearings or markers which assist the historian in making his way through the dense mass of his material.

Thus generalizations like 'economic changes in society are accompanied by religious changes' have a looseness we do not associate with the laws formulated in sciences like physics, chemistry, or even biology. The concepts 'economic change', 'religious change' are vague and complex. Will any degree of economic change, however slight, be sufficient to bring about a religious change? And, if not, how much is required? And of what kind must it be? One is inclined to say that generalizations of the kind in question provide indications, and rough ones at that, of the sorts of factors which, under certain circumstances, we expect to find correlated with other sorts of factors; but that they leave open to historical investigation and analysis the task of eliciting the specific nature of those factors on a particular occasion, and the precise manner in which the factors are causally connected with one another. And, this being so, we may also feel that to talk in this context of 'laws', and of the 'application' of laws, is inappropriate. For to speak of 'laws' here may lead us to forget or neglect features that are important. And it is those that I wish to stress.

There is, in fact, more than one level of imprecision

---

[1] See Felix Kaufmann, *Methodology of the Social Sciences*, particularly chap. xiii·

involved in the historian's generalizations. Not only is there a wide and indefinite *ceteris paribus* clause presupposed by their formulation. They are also imprecise in that the terms which are employed in their statement have an 'openness' of the type discussed above which precludes any attempt to demarcate precisely the area of their application. Nor is it implied that they *always* hold: compare everyday generalizations like 'people fear death' and 'love is blind', which would not be regarded as having been falsified by someone who showed that there are exceptions.

To bring out the use of such generalizations in history, it may be illuminating to consider an analogous case drawn from a different field. Consider those judgements that are made in the face of situations demanding a practical decision. Generals before launching an offensive, statesmen before initiating a policy, are said to 'appreciate the situation' in which action is contemplated. A particular decision taken, or course of action embarked upon, is said in general to be justified if the agent is able to produce reasons describing factors in the situation confronting him which, considered together and *ceteris paribus*, strongly *suggest* or *support* the conclusion that the course of action he contemplates will be successful in achieving the end he desires. And again, in such a case, it would be unreasonable to demand that, for the course of action decided upon to be termed justified, the agent should give reasons that exhibited the elements in the situation as values of precisely formulated invariant laws. For this demand would represent a misunderstanding of the logic of practical choice. A request for the specification of *precise* rules is not in point here. The rules of military strategy, for instance, if it be allowed that they are 'rules' at all, are such that they permit a wide margin for their possible interpretation when they are considered in connexion with any particular contingency. A general might refer to a certain strategic precept as one which upon most occasions can be relied upon to succeed but which, under exceptional circumstances, may lead to catastrophe. He might go on to specify the nature of those circumstances, although he need not, and probably would not, do more than indicate them very roughly; nor is it likely that he would attempt to draw any sharp line between those circumstances and the circumstances under which the rule might be expected to be effective. It might, indeed, be said that it is in the making of decisions of just this type, where the borderline is vague and indefinite between circumstances favourable to the success of an applied rule and circumstances favourable to its failure, that the quality of generalship is manifested: a general is not a good general because he knows, for example, Clausewitz by heart: he may, on the other hand, be a good one because he applies Clausewitz's principles with intelligence and flexibility.

The historian, like the general or the statesman, tends to *assess* rather than to *conclude*. As has been said in a valuable contribution to a related problem:[1] '. . . the historian is not primarily concerned to establish general statements falsifiable by experiment, but . . . his conclusions (if any) are judgements about particular persons and particular events', and 'it is the distinguishing characteristic of practical and historical judgements (as opposed to statements of fact and scientific statements) that the conditions of their falsification are not exactly prescribed'. There is, indeed, a point in terming (for example) the explanations provided by the historian 'judgements', although it is not to be supposed that by thus naming them we are implying that they are 'subjective' in any vicious sense. For the word 'judgement' must be regarded as being in the nature of a technical term the function of which in this context is to indicate, not that historical accounts of why particular events occurred are inadequate, conjectural, or 'phoney', but simply that the criteria for assessing the validity of any given explanation in history are, in general, different from those appropriate to the assessment of explanations as they occur in certain branches of scientific inquiry. Nor would it be correct to say that historical judgements are made, or accepted, in default of anything 'better': we should rather insist that their

[1] Stuart Hampshire, 'Subjunctive Conditionals', *Analysis*, Oct. 1948.

formulation represents the *end* of historical inquiry, not that they are stages on the journey towards that end.

In the light of this we can perhaps see more clearly why it is artificial and misleading to suggest that explanations in history represent sequences of events as instantiating cases of laws which can be exhibited tidily and comprehensively and for which there exist precise rules of application. In this respect the pattern taken (or rather not taken) by historical arguments is significant. A postulated historical explanation is not, as a rule, justified (or challenged) by demonstrating that a given law implied by it does (or does not) hold; far less by showing such a law to follow (or not to follow) from an accepted theory or hypothesis, or to be confirmed (or falsified) by experiment; nor, again, by pointing out that the case under consideration does (or does not) satisfy in the required respects the conditions exactly specified in the formulation of the law.

And we can understand why, instead, the historian is likely to insist that, fully to comprehend the explanations he provides, the events that concern him must be considered in all their detail and complexity. The direction of history is from the general to the particular. Faced by the question: 'Why did Louis XIV die unpopular?' we can visualize the historian reasoning as follows: 'As a general precept we may take it as true that rulers of countries who pursue policies detrimental to the countries over which they rule become unpopular. Did this hold in the case of Louis XIV?'

He will then proceed to examine Louis XIV's policy under its various aspects while at the same time taking into consideration other features of the reign that might render the hypothesis untenable or suggest an alternative interpretation of the facts. And he may conclude his investigations by expressing the judgement that Louis XIV did, in fact, die unpopular because the policy he pursued was detrimental to the French nation, and that, if he had pursued a different policy, his status amongst his subjects at the end of his reign would have been different also.

We should by now be clear why the historian hedges when

it is suggested to him that Louis XIV's unpopularity is a case of the law that rulers become unpopular when they pursue certain sorts of policy. For although there is a sense in which it is true that when he is giving his explanation it is some such generalization that he has in mind, it is only as a result of an elaborate assessment of the various factors involved in the particular case before him that he is enabled to give his verdict. And it is for these reasons that we are inclined to say that his explanation is in the nature of a sketch that requires 'filling in'. Just as the historian opens his inquiry by using the hypothesis as a guide, so the explanation he gives at its close may be interpreted as pointing to the directions in which, to use Hempel's terminology, confirmation may be found.

There is something odd about speaking of an explanation being 'confirmed': laws, it may be objected, are confirmed, but not explanations. Explanations are 'justified' or 'supported'. Supporting an historical explanation of the type we are considering consists in telling more of the story. And this requires further specification of the factors involved. We can conceive of an historian, when challenged by an objector, replying: 'If you do not believe my explanation, take a closer look at the facts. Consider Louis's disastrous wars, his extravagance, his court policy. Consider, too, the favourable position in which the country was placed at the beginning of his reign. As a result of such a situation, would you not expect a king to die unpopular?' And, if asked to be even more explicit, he might go on to show the effects which the various factors he has mentioned had upon the different sections of the French population.[1] In this way, the explanation, formerly vague and 'open', is given body and weight. But this is not to say that in its original form it was worthless or empirically meaningless; for we know roughly the kind of factors which would lead us to say that it was or was not justified, these factors being such that, when they have been specified, they can be seen to satisfy the antecedent of a general hypothetical indicating the general

---

[1] Which again, of course, are causal statements, although of a more specific nature.

H

character of the conditions under which rulers become unpopular. I say 'general character of the conditions' advisedly,
for it is precisely this feature of historical explanation that
differentiates it from scientific explanation in the way we have
described, and that inclines us to say the historian's statements are 'judgements' or 'interpretations'. Here, indeed, is
an important point, but it is equally important to recognize
that the character of historical explanations is not such as to
allow us, when analysing them, to dispense with all reference
to laws, of whatever type, and to content ourselves, simply
and solely, with 'the facts'. For how then is the force of the
'because' to be accounted for, unless we fall back once more
upon the notion of individual and 'intuitable' connexions, a
notion with which we have found good reasons to quarrel?

To summarize. That historical explanation is often an
extremely complicated affair has not been denied. Nor has it
been denied that to explain particular historical events frequently requires a lengthy and detailed analysis of the individual case. But I have tried to show that one of the reasons why
a similar analysis is not requisite in scientific explanation is
that there are prescribed tests in most sciences whereby it can
be decided whether or not a particular event satisfies a precisely formulated law. On the level of common sense, although
the margins are wider, the conditions under which a generalization may be expected to hold less explicitly stated, we are not
usually in doubt about the possible effects of bricks striking
windows or billiard-balls colliding. Historical situations present a multitude of interrelated factors whose relevance or
irrelevance to the events we wish to explain is difficult to
determine. The more complex the events dealt with, the wider
their spread in time and space, the greater are the calls made
upon the historian's judgement.[1] Further, it is usually the
case that not one, but many, generalizations of the type we

[1] A point often ignored. Philosophers tend to talk as if all historical explanation took place upon the same level of generality. For a discussion of this, see
A. M. MacIver's contribution to the symposium 'The Character of an Historical
Explanation', in the *Proceedings of the Aristotelian Society*, supplementary,
vol. xxi.

have been considering must be used to guide the historian in his quest; it is rarely true that he reaches his conclusion by presupposing one simple law of the kind instanced in our quotation from Popper. Historians offer several causes for an event of any degree of magnitude or complexity.

There is thus a 'slide' from explanation as it occurs in science to explanation as it occurs in history. We can, if we wish, say that the difference is only one of degree, but we must be careful. We can say this if what we mean to emphasize is the fact that historical explanation presupposes regularity, that it involves a knowledge of how things and people in general behave which can be, and at times is, made more explicit—what Bradley called 'the character of our general consciousness'. It is important, nevertheless, to remember that historical explanation is in many ways a curious affair. We might, without being too misleading, perhaps compare it to a game where there is no clearly formulated set of rules; the more we try to tighten the rules, the more difficult it is to play the game. The pieces, too, display a bewildering variety: some are hard and concrete, we can see them and touch them; but others hover like will-o'-the-wisps before our vision, and, when we inspect them too closely, disappear altogether from sight. This may be a far-fetched picture: but perhaps after all we should not be so very surprised, or so very shocked, when philosophers tell us that history is *sui generis*, an autonomous branch of study; although we may indeed legitimately disagree with many of the grounds upon which they have based their claim.

§ 4. *Cause and Context in History*

AT the close of the last section it was mentioned that the different levels of generality upon which historical explanation takes place is a fact frequently ignored in discussions of the subject. We must now consider in more detail how a disregard of the contextual reference of 'cause' and kindred terms may lead to the generation of seemingly insoluble puzzles. My treatment will at best be sketchy, as a lengthy analysis would absorb more space than I have at my disposal; I shall confine myself to attempting to uncover the principal sources of the problems.

First, the puzzles.

These cluster round such forms of expression as 'the true cause of y was x', 'the most important cause of y was x', 'the immediate cause of y was x', 'x was not the real cause of y', 'but for the occurrence of the unforeseeable (accidental, chance) event x, y would not have occurred'. All these are common enough expressions and can be found in any history book: nevertheless, they are prone to give rise to heated arguments, especially amongst those who speculate about the historical process as a whole. Thus, statements like the following are made:

1. '. . . the economic relations, however much they may be influenced by the other political and ideological ones, are still ultimately the decisive ones, forming the red thread which runs through them and alone leads to understanding. . . . In default of a Napoleon, another would have filled his place, that is established by the fact that, whenever a man was necessary, he has always been found . . .'[1]

2. 'Why was the fate of France in the hands of a man who totally lacked the ability and desire to save society? Because such was the form of organization of that society.'[2]

3. 'Indeed, it is necessary to recognize as one of the principles of any unprejudiced view of politics that everything is possible in human affairs: and more particularly that no conceivable development can be excluded on the grounds that it may violate the so-called tendency of human progress, or any other of the alleged laws of "human nature".'[3]

4. 'The mutations of society, then, from generation to generation, are in the main due directly or indirectly to the acts or examples of individuals whose genius was . . . adapted to the receptivities of the moment.'[4]

Roughly (1) and (2) are statements that fall on one side of the fence, and (3) and (4) statements that fall on the other,

[1] Engels in a letter to Heinz Starkenburg, 25 Jan. 1894.
[2] Plekhanov, *The Rôle of the Individual in History*, p. 41.
[3] K. R. Popper, op. cit., vol. ii, p. 185.
[4] William James, 'Great Men and their Environment', *Atlantic Monthly*, Oct. 1880.

opposing, side. Both sides support their contentions by evidence; yet however long the argument lasts and however much evidence is collected on both sides to back up the opposing theses, little progress is made towards reaching a settlement of the dispute. And in such circumstances it is appropriate to ask whether the debate concerns a genuine issue.

When an historian asserts (as he is prone to assert) a statement of the form 'the true cause of y was x', how is this statement to be interpreted?

In common life, as has already been pointed out (Part I, § 3), to give the cause of an event is to select one from a number of conditions; for example, we often call 'the cause' of an event that condition which enables us to produce or prevent that event. Thus we should call the cause of an explosion the ignition of the gunpowder, but we do not thereby imply that a number of other conditions need not have been present if the gunpowder was to explode; although a necessary condition, ignition is not by itself a sufficient condition of gunpowder's exploding.

We do not, however, always confine ourselves to saying that such-and-such was 'the cause' of an event: there are occasions when we speak of 'root' or 'real' causes. The precise meaning to be given to such expressions is difficult to determine owing to the wide variety of contexts in which they may occur. Consider:

1. 'Jones says it's because he ate parsnips for lunch, but, of course, the *real cause* is the party he went to last night.'

2. 'It wasn't what you said just then that *really made* him flare up: he hasn't forgotten what you said about him last week.'

3. 'The police may have caught the perpetrators of the outrages, but they are mere puppets. The *true cause* lies deeper; we must find out who is *behind* this criminal organization.'

4. 'The *root cause* of the trouble is not the strikers' behaviour—it's Moscow.'

5. 'He says he is doing it to strike a blow for peace, but his
   real reason is the desire to further the interests of his
   class.'

In (1) the suggestion is that, although it may be true that
Jones would not have suffered from indigestion if he had not
eaten parsnips at lunch, nevertheless he would not have
suffered (however many parsnips he might have eaten) if he
had not consumed alcohol the night before. The alcohol-
cause is considered to be 'deeper' than the parsnip-cause, not
because the alcohol alone was sufficient to bring about the
attack of indigestion—the statement does not necessarily imply
this—but because on normal occasions, i.e. when Jones is not
suffering from a hangover, parsnips do not give him indigestion. And the selection of the 'real cause' from the conditions
believed to determine Jones's indigestion is thus made from
a point of view which presupposes the normal functioning of
Jones's digestive processes. For let us suppose that Jones's
digestion is working normally and that he unwittingly takes
arsenic. We should not then say: 'You are wrong to say the
cause of Jones's pains is his taking arsenic: the *real cause* is the
way his digestion works', although, of course, the fact that Jones
is unable to digest arsenic is a condition of his having pains.

In (2) the suggestion is again that in normal circumstances
the man referred to would not have been angry at the remark
addressed to him, and it is with the criterion of how he would
have behaved under normal circumstances that the judgement is made that the real cause of his display of temper was
his memory of what was said on a previous occasion. Nevertheless, it is not implied thereby that he would have lost his
temper at the precise time at which he did if the remark in
question (or one like it) had not been made. And if the man
was *in the habit* of losing his temper when remarks of the
type made were addressed to him, we should not make the
distinction.

In (3) the criterion of the 'true cause' is a pragmatic one.
If the police arrest Smith and Jones, will the disturbances
cease? If not, then they do not represent the cause in question,

although it may be absurd to deny that it was their activities which caused the crimes that have so far been committed. And again with (4): if the strikers' grievances (which may be legitimate ones) are met, will labour troubles cease?

(5) is, however, rather different. For here, not a cause, but a reason is being given which is rejected. We have 'seen through' the reason offered by a man for his conduct to what is believed to be the reason which really leads him to act as he does.

Thus the expression 'real cause' is used in the explanations (1)–(4) in order to contrast one of the conditions present with other conditions for some particular reason. In ordinary speech, the contrast is often driven home by terming such other conditions 'immediate causes' or 'occasions' and by using words like 'symptoms', 'signs', &c. For example, 'the *occasion* of Jones's pains was the parsnips he ate at lunch', 'the *immediate cause* of his losing his temper was your remark', 'Smith and Brown were *instrumental* in causing the damage', 'the strikers' behaviour is *symptomatic of* the activities of Moscow'.

I have considered these examples from common speech because they throw light upon the use of similar expressions in history. Historians speak of 'fundamental causes', of 'deep-rooted forces', of 'developments which rendered such-and-such a phenomenon in the long run inevitable'. And there is a tendency to suppose that these 'rock-bottom' causes in some sense invalidate or render suspect other causes that may be referred to as explaining historical events.[1] And this in turn leads to arguments of the kind we have mentioned where it is suggested, for instance, that 'material' forces or 'National Spirits' on the one hand, or human wills, on the other, determine the total development of history. The question is: which? And it may be supposed that when this question is answered and we know the Prime Mover, all the rest will automatically follow, unfolding like a wonderful plant emerging from its magic seed.[2] Empirical inquiry can cease, and historians

---

[1] Cf. Plekhanov, *In Defence of Materialism*, passim.

[2] This is Hegel's own simile: 'We may compare it [the National Spirit] with the seed; for with this the plant begins . . .', *The Philosophy of History*, p. 78.

can more profitably devote themselves instead to a close inspection of the mechanism which makes things happen as they do.

But these 'theories' have their source in an incorrect interpretation of historical explanations of the 'root cause' type. The suggestion seems to be that when an historian terms x the 'real cause' of y, he has in some mysterious way seen the quality of 'realness' stamped upon it, and has been able to pick it out by means of this piece of insight. This also accounts for the belief that all 'true causes' in history must be of one type, e.g. economic, ideological, and so forth.

But in common life, as we have seen, to term one event the 'true cause' of another event entails no such consequence. What may be called 'the true cause' in one context may not be so called in another. In the case of the man who has indigestion after eating parsnips, we may refer to his hangover as the 'true cause'. But let us imagine the case of another man who is a dipsomaniac and who has a hangover every day, so that his digestion is constantly unsatisfactory. Supposing this man eats parsnips for lunch and consequently feels unwell. Should we, when confronted with such a state of affairs, feel inclined to say that the true cause of his feeling ill was his having consumed an excessive quantity of alcohol the night before? Suppose that we took a kindly view of his dipsomania and regarded it as incurable, part of his make-up, should we not be more likely to say something like: 'Eating parsnips—that's his trouble. He'd better give it up?'

Moreover, in such cases, we do not think that there is necessarily a contradiction between two explanations of the form 'x was the cause of y' and 'z was the real (actual) cause of y'. For the statement 'y would not have happened if x had not happened, but z was the real cause, nevertheless' is obviously consistent.

In history where a very large number of conditions are either stated or are assumed to hold when an historical explanation is offered, the choice of a particular condition as the 'true cause' frequently occurs. But the choice is not dictated by a mysterious property belonging to one of the conditions which somehow sets it above all the rest, although the writings of some theorists suggest that this is the case.

Analysis of historical explanations of the 'true cause' type would reveal, not the apprehension of special properties belonging to all events termed 'real causes', but the point of view of the historian, the level of generality upon which he is speaking. An historian asserts that the murder of the Austrian archduke was not the real cause of the First World War. A journalist, on the other hand, writing a leader just after war has been declared, may sum up the situation in different terms: for him the origin of the war *will* lie in the incident at Sarajevo. And this will be because his interest, his viewpoint, is limited to the period of intense diplomatic activity that led up to the outbreak of hostilities. By speaking of the Sarajevo incident as the cause of the war he means, for instance, that without Sarajevo the mobilization of the Austrian armies and the counter-mobilization of the Russian armies would not have taken place at the time and in the order they did, that without taking Sarajevo into account the entire pattern of the diplomacy which preceded war would be inexplicable. Writing within this context, the journalist is justified in speaking of Sarajevo as the root cause, the fundamental factor, with reference to which the rest may be explained.

It is, therefore, a mistake to imagine that the historian is contradicting the journalist when he says that the Sarajevo assassination was not the true cause of the outbreak of the First World War. He is merely regarding the outbreak of war from a different point of view, talking about it upon a different level. The question 'Why did the First World War occur?' is answerable in various ways: it is answerable upon the level of individual human purposes, desires, weaknesses, and abilities; it is answerable upon the level of national policies, traditions of diplomacy, plans; it is answerable upon the level of political alignments, treaties, the international structure of Europe in 1914; it is answerable upon the level of economic trends, social organization, political doctrine, ideology, and the rest. And it is interesting to note that the looseness of the concepts employed serves to hide such distinctions and to blur their significance. When, for example, it is asked: 'What were the real causes of the First World War?' is the question to be interpreted as a request for information concerning why it was that the First World War broke out upon August the Fourth 1914 rather than at any other time, or is it to be interpreted as a request for information as to why it broke out at all, what were the nature of the conditions that made it likely that a war would break out at some time during the first twenty years of the twentieth century even if the Sarajevo incident had never taken place? ('Even if he had not eaten parsnips for lunch, the chestnuts he was going to have at tea might have done the trick.') It is part of the function of expressions like 'real cause' to make it clear upon what level the question is being answered and how, for example, the words 'the First World War' are being interpreted.

The implications of an historian's use of the word 'cause' in a particular connexion can frequently be illuminated by translating the explanation in question into a different grammatical form, the form of the contrary-to-fact conditional. This is brought out in Raymond Aron's *Introduction à la Philosophie de l'Histoire*.[1] 'Examinons', he writes,

> le cas de la Révolution de 1848: elle a eu pour *cause immédiate*, selon l'expression courante, les coups de feu sur les boulevards. Nul ne met en doute cette consécution. Mais certains diminuent l'importance des derniers incidents en affirmant que si ceux-ci n'avaient pas eu lieu, la Révolution n'en aurait moins éclaté. Cette affirmation, exprimée rigoureusement, équivaut à la proposition: en supprimant (par la pensée) les coups de feu, les autres antécédents, dans leur ensemble, sont cause adéquate d'une révolution. Au contraire, si un historien pense que la situation rendait possible, mais non probable, une révolution, l'efficace des coups de feu en grandira d'autant. Enfin la révolution sera accidentelle par rapport à la situation si, dans le plus grand nombre des cas, elle ne se produit pas. . . . Un antécédent immédiat n'est que *l'occasion* d'un évènement lorsque, aux yeux de l'historien, l'évènement considéré devait inévitablement se produire étant donnée la situation historique.

Thus, suppose an historian tells us that the shots on the

[1] p. 165.

boulevards caused the 1848 Revolution, and we proceed to translate his statement so that it reads:

1. 'If the shots on the boulevards had not occurred, the revolution would not have occurred.'

Confronted by this translation the historian might feel indignant. He might object that he did not wish to say anything as extreme as this, that the revolution would have happened anyway even if the shots had not occurred, that they were only the *occasion* of its occurrence, and so forth. Accordingly, we may ask him whether he means:

2. 'If the shots on the boulevards had not occurred, the revolution would not have occurred at the time at which and in the form in which it did occur (e.g. taken a different course, been crushed at the start, led to the victory of the proletariat, &c.).' Or:

3. 'If the shots on the boulevards had not occurred, the revolution would not have occurred at the precise time at which it did occur, although it would otherwise have followed approximately the same course.'

It is evident that (2) is weaker than (1) and (3) is weaker than (2). Yet (1), (2), and (3) are all consistent with the original statement that the shots on the boulevards caused the Revolution of 1848: what they do is to make it more explicit, while at the same time showing how slippery is the word 'cause', especially when it is used in contexts where the other concepts employed are open to various interpretations. And they help to bring out more clearly the function of epithets like 'real', 'partial', 'immediate', 'accidental', when these qualify the mention of 'causes'.

Many, apparently insoluble, problems arise because of the indefiniteness of the questions asked, because they occur without reference to any particular context or to any rules according to which an answer may be provided. 'Was the rise of Hitler really the cause of the Second World War or would it have occurred without him?' 'Can we say that the fact that Stalin and not Trotsky succeeded Lenin in Russia caused the

Soviet state to develop as it did during the succeeding decades?' The common feeling is that we find these questions difficult to answer because of a lack of knowledge, because of certain empirical snags. I suggest, however, that this is not the principal reason: for what such questions do is to hustle us (and the historian) into giving answers to which, owing to the form the questions take, there will always and necessarily be room for objections. The formulation of the questions makes them appear as if they were of the same type as unambiguous questions like 'Who escaped from Elba?' where to give the name of a single individual is to provide a satisfactory answer.

In fact, they are incomplete. 'Were shots on the boulevards the cause of the 1848 Revolution in France?' Does this mean: 'Would the Revolution have broken out at the precise time at which it did break out if they had not occurred?' Or does it mean: 'Would the Revolution have broken out sooner or later even if there had been no shots?' And if, after receiving an affirmative answer to the latter question, we ask: 'What then was the real cause of the Revolution?', further specification is again required. For there are a number of possible answers. Which is picked out, which is chosen, is dependent upon the point of view from which the event under examination is being considered. Are we interested in the programme that was announced by the revolutionaries? In that case, the 'intellectual currents', the 'climate of opinion', of the pre-1848 period will be relevant. Are we interested in why 'a grotesque mediocrity' was able 'to strut about in a hero's garb'? In that case, the alignments and relative strength of the social classes in the France of 1848 may be of importance.

It is, of course, a mistake to suppose that the historian is always bent upon answering questions of this type, that his task is always to quest after 'the true cause' in any situation. To suggest that this is the case is to disregard the evidence of history books. Open any history book: what will you find? 'The causes of so-and-so were . . .', 'One of the causes of so-and-so was . . .' And this is a consequence of the extreme complexity of the situations that confront the historian, which, as we have seen, makes the decision as to whether, and, if so, to what extent, one event was caused by another event so hard to determine, and thus tests his judgement. In so far, however, as a choice from amongst the conditioning factors *is* made, in so far as some are termed 'fundamental' or 'primary', others 'contributory' or 'secondary', it is to the standpoint of the historian that we must turn if we wish to interpret correctly what is being asserted.

The bearing of what has been said upon apparently insoluble arguments as to what is really *behind* the historical process, what makes the machine work and the wheels go round, should by now be clear. Misled by the ambiguities hidden in the word 'cause', philosophers have believed that somewhere in every historical situation there is present a factor of a certain type and that, once this factor is pin-pointed, everything else can be seen to follow from it. But this belief is an illusion. The historical process is not like a machine that has to be kept in motion by a metaphysical dynamo behind the scenes. And there are no absolute Real Causes waiting to be discovered by historians with sufficiently powerful magnifying-glasses. What do exist are historians writing upon different levels and at different distances, historians writing with different aims and different interests, historians writing in different contexts and from different points of view. It is not altogether surprising that, when the levels are confused, the contextual distinctions blurred, and the points of view run into one another, contradictions arise and antinomies are created. For when this is done there are no rules according to which the dispute may be settled.

It may be objected that I am ignoring the facts, and that when Marxian historians assert that history is explicable in terms of economic relations they are affirming a proposition that has had an immense and fruitful influence upon the writing of history. But this truth can be accepted without our being forced thereby to accept the Real Cause story, or Engels' fairy-tale of substitute-Napoleons. When Engels informs us that 'the economic relations . . . are . . . ultimately the decisive ones' we are obliged to ask him for an elucidation of the expression 'ultimately decisive'. What, we may legitimately inquire, do they decide? Everything? Engels equivocates; he writes: 'That such-and-such a man and precisely that man arrives at that particular time in that given country is, of course, pure accident', but he immediately adds: 'but cut him out and there will be a demand for a substitute, and this substitute will be found, good or bad, but in the long run he will be found . . . this is established by the fact that whenever a man was necessary, he has always been found'.

Now this is an illuminating statement, illuminating because it shows where the search for the Grail of Real Causes ends—in bad metaphysics. For it is clear that Engels' assertion that a great man will always be found when he is needed (by whom? society? the historical process?) is irrefutable only in the sense that nothing would ever count against it. For what is the criterion for deciding whether or not a great man is necessary? Whether or not he emerges. And however much a particular situation may seem to require the presence of a great man, in any ordinary meaning of 'require', Engels can always explain the fact that a great man has not appeared by saying that all this proves is that a great man was not 'really necessary'. Engels can never be proved wrong, but nobody is left any the wiser for that.

In emphasizing the role played by economic factors in history, Marxian historians may be justified. And in a particular situation it may be correct to say that economic factors were 'decisive', when it is made clear what precisely this means. Thus we may perhaps say that economic factors were responsible for Napoleon's rise to power if by this it is meant that, if the economic situation of France had not been what it was at the close of the eighteenth century, a man of Napoleon's calibre and abilities would not have been able to take his opportunity. But to assert this is in no sense to assert that, if no Napoleon had existed, there would necessarily have been another man ready to seize the opportunity which circumstances offered. Economic conditions do not *create* Napoleons;

they merely provide them with their openings. Circumstances are a necessary condition of the rise of a great man: they are not a sufficient condition.

Similar muddles occur when it is said that history is the story of individual initiative or of chance. 'Everything is possible in human affairs.' If what this means is that situations arise wherein human beings are presented with two or more alternative courses of action between which they are at liberty to choose, there can be no quarrel. We can say: 'It was open to Napoleon not to have tried to escape from Elba'. But can we say: 'It was open to Napoleon to have reconquered the continent of Europe'? Many historians would deny that it was so open to him. The use of the word 'possible', like the use of the expression 'decisive cause', requires a context, a point of view, before rational discussion can begin.

Likewise with 'chance'. We know what it means to say that something-or-other happened 'by chance'. But we feel baffled when we are told that it is the god of Chance who rules the destinies of men. There is a tendency to present us with the following disjunction: either history is governed by the 'blind play of Chance' or it is governed by the 'iron laws' of an inexorable necessity.[1] But J. B. Bury, whose essay 'Cleopatra's Nose' is an example of what may be termed the 'chance' or 'contingency' theory of history, was far from hypostatizing chance in this way, insisting that 'we must have a proper view of chance' and that we must not regard it as 'the intrusion of a lawless element'. Chance means 'the valuable collision of two or more independent chains of causes'. Was it by chance that Jones had indigestion after lunch on Thursday? It was, when by this it is meant that if, instead of parsnips, peas had been on the menu, Jones would not have had indigestion. But it is not by chance that he had indigestion, if by this it is meant that Jones's indigestion was not causally explicable. Was it by chance that Napoleon came to power in France?

[1] See Arnold Toynbee, *Civilisation on Trial*, chap. i: 'If a vehicle is to move forward on a course which its driver has set, it must be borne along on wheels that turn monotonously round and round.' The wheels are presumably 'civilizations'.

If by this it is meant that he would not have come to power if he had not been born or if he had not been trained as a soldier, then we may say that it was. But to speak of 'chance' in this way always involves reference to particular causal sequences: an event may be 'chance' relative to one sequence, but not necessarily 'chance' relative to another sequence. To labour the point further would be tedious.

In this section I have been concerned to show how some of the ways in which 'cause' and associated terms are used in history may lead to illegitimate conclusions regarding the procedure of the historian. I have not been concerned to deny the success that historical 'theories' like the Marxian may have achieved in emphasizing factors previously ignored by historians, and in bringing to light previously unsuspected correlations between different aspects of social development. Theories of this kind may indeed be regarded in some respects as 'pointers' to types of historical material which may prove relevant to the understanding of a particular historical situation, from a certain angle and for certain purposes. But they do not, I think, function like scientific theories: their significance lies in their suggestive power, their directive importance.[1] And while upon certain levels of historical inquiry their application may prove fertile and illuminating, upon others it may be merely a source of distortion and confusion.

[1] A point worth emphasizing in view of the harsh treatment generally meted out to historical 'interpretations' by modern empiricists. For instance, Hempel, in the article already quoted above, writes: 'The interpretations which are actually offered in history consist either in subsuming the phenomena in question under a scientific explanation or explanation sketch; or in an attempt to subsume them under some general idea which is not amenable to any empirical test. . . . The latter . . . amounts to a pseudo-explanation which may have emotive appeal and evoke vivid pictorial associations, but which does not further our theoretical understanding of the phenomena under consideration.' As Hempel does not in this passage give examples of what he means, it is difficult to criticize him. But in any case his attack is too sweeping. Can we not distinguish in importance between one historical interpretation which involves, say, a theory of racial destiny or of historical justice, and another which involves, perhaps, a theory of economic causation? (Even Hegelian talk of 'National Spirits' may be illuminating, emphasizing as it does the importance of examining the inter-relationship between various aspects of a community's life at a given time. But we must be careful to separate the ore from the dross.)

PART IV

SOME OTHER ASPECTS OF HISTORICAL EXPLANATION

§ 1. *Introductory*

UP to now we have been concerned to consider the extent to which it is possible to regard historical explanation as conforming to the pattern outlined in the opening section of this book entitled 'The Logic of Explanation'. It was, however, there emphasized that it is mistaken to presume, as many empiricists have been wont to do, that all explanation works to this pattern. And we have already drawn attention to some examples of historical explanation that do not appear to do so. Further, it was pointed out in Part II, § 4, that the difficulty of accommodating explanations of the types in question has been taken as a fundamental reason for arguing that historical explanation is *sui generis*, with its own unique logic and procedure.

The problems that arise in this connexion are multifold, and a full consideration of them would take us far outside the scope of the present work. Accordingly, in the space still at my disposal I propose to limit myself to trying to answer some of the more insistent of the questions that are likely to be raised at this stage. And my task will not be made easier by the fact that I desire at the same time to do justice to a view which, as it has ordinarily been stated, would appear at first sight to conflict with the interpretation of historical explanation that has been offered above. To show that no such conflict need in fact occur will be one object of the argument to be developed in this section: and much that I have to say will for this reason be a development and expansion of some of the points already raised.

As the topic is one of some complexity, I shall adopt the following procedure:

1. Present the problem of the part played in historical

explanation by what are usually called 'mental events' or 'mental acts' as it has frequently been stated by philosophers, and sketch briefly the kind of answer they have given and the consequences for historical method that have been alleged to follow from it. (In setting this out, I shall inevitably have to recapitulate something of what has already been said.)

2. Try to disentangle some of the beliefs presupposed in this view, taking each on its merits, and asking (a) to what extent it is true, and (b) what consequences can legitimately be inferred from it.

3. Consider what bearing the conclusions thus reached have upon the answer to the original problem.

§ 2. *The Problem of 'Mental Causation'*

HISTORIANS do not, as we have seen, confine themselves to giving explanations of human actions which refer to various types of what might be called 'physical' or 'publicly observable' events, such as, for example, the actions of other human beings, earthquakes, cold winters, the publication of proclamations, and so forth. When they do give explanations of this kind, we have argued that their procedure presupposes the assumption of causal laws, that is, their explanations may be analysed in terms of observed regularities between events. But in history, as well as in ordinary life, explanations are also given that seem to be different: we come across statements of the form 'x did y in order to achieve z', 'x intended to achieve z, therefore he did y', 'x did y because he desired z', 'x's ambition explains his doing y', and 'x did y because he thought that if he didn't, w would do z'. Historians, in fact, in many of their explanations of human conduct make reference to the intentions, desires, thoughts, plans, and policies of the people in whom they are interested.

It is here that the central problem of historical writing is alleged to arise. It would be foolish to deny the importance of this kind of explanation. Moreover, it is a form of explanation which is primarily used with reference to the activities of human beings. It makes nonsense to speak of certain kinds of natural phenomena being motivated or having desires: Newton's apple did not fall to the ground because it desired to do so, and volcanoes, when they erupt, do not erupt with the intention of destroying the inhabitants who live upon their slopes. The planets do not move in their courses because they want to avoid disturbing the smooth workings of the solar system. With forms of life, the distinction is harder to draw: but there is a sensation of uneasiness, a feeling that language is being subtly misused, when we are told that bees store honey in order to provide for the winter, or that the cat is walking to the window because it plans to go out. This kind of language, we want to say, is only unambiguously applicable when we are discussing the actions of human beings. It is only when we are speaking of men and their doings that it is strictly correct to use words like 'intention', 'belief', 'thought', and 'plan'.

Now history is the study of what *human beings* have done. Hence, it is argued, the type of explanation referred to above assumes in history a major significance. Upon this very point centres the crucial distinction between history and natural science. The distinction is stated as follows by Collingwood:

> When a scientist asks 'Why did that piece of litmus paper turn pink?' he means 'On what kinds of occasions do pieces of litmus paper turn pink?' When an historian asks 'Why did Brutus stab Caesar?' he means 'What did Brutus think, which made him decide to stab Caesar?' The cause of the event, for him, means the thought in the mind of the person by whose agency the event came about . . .[1]

Given that this distinction between history and natural science is correct, it is then argued that the principal problem to which the philosopher of history must find a solution is the problem (*a*) of describing in what precisely consists this special form of causation with which the historian is concerned, (*b*) of showing in what sense the historian can be said to know what, in a particular case, caused an historical figure to act as he did.

[1] *Idea of History*, pp. 214–15.

I have already outlined the answers that Collingwood gives to these two questions; let me briefly recapitulate, emphasizing certain features. In answer to (1) above, it is held that to assert that it was somebody's motive or intention or plan to do something is to talk about a mental event which precedes or 'lies behind' or, again, 'lies within', the action to which it gives rise. It is not difficult to see the reasons why this view has been favoured. Much of our talk about motives and intentions resembles our talk about causes and effects, and suggests that the type of inference involved when we say, for example, that the cigarette ash, the state of the tea things, and the overcoat hanging in the hall are evidence for Smith's being at home is the same as the type of inference involved when we say that Jones's cryptic references to Smith at dinner are evidence for the fact that he intends to murder Smith. In this way, a word like 'motive' or 'intention' is taken to refer to an entity of a non-physical or 'mental' kind, and it is the existence of this entity which gives the agent the necessary 'push' that makes him act.

If this is the case, the second aspect of our problem, namely, in what sense an historian may be said to know what made a person act as he did, presents a peculiar difficulty. Whereas in the case of ordinary cause–effect inference we are confronted with events that are at any rate in principle observable, in the case of explanations in terms of thoughts and intentions the entity whose existence we infer in order to explain the action that interests us is in principle unobservable: it does not even appear to make sense to say that we can *observe* another person's motives. The motives of other people are not like performing-bears in a circus-ring. Under what conditions, then, are we justified in saying that we know what another person's motives were, since we can never be presented with a case where both the motive for another person's action and the action which followed upon it are present in our experience?

A possible answer to this question is that our knowledge is justified on analogy with our own experience. From the fact that we ourselves have motives which are followed by our performing certain actions, we infer, when we observe people performing similar actions, that their motives are similar to our own when we perform those actions. Stated thus, however, there are objections to this view; and it is in any case unpalatable to those theorists who wish to insist that historical thinking is unlike the procedure of natural scientists, since it would once again open the door to an interpretation of historical explanation in terms of regularities or laws—in this case between 'mental events' and physical actions. Therefore an alternative story is told. It is suggested that it is possible to have the *same* thought as another person;[1] and, if this is so, the difficulty disappears. We can know *why* somebody did something just as 'directly' as we can know *what* it was that he did. There is no inference to unobservable 'interior' mental events: it is indeed suggested that there is no inference at all. 'Inference', as the word is frequently employed in ordinary speech, is taken to mean the assertion of the existence of one event on the ground of the known existence of another event in virtue of a causal law. The main force of what has been called the 'inside-outside theory' of human action resides in the claim that it is incorrect to say that a human action consists merely of certain physical movements from which we *infer* the motive 'behind it'; it consists of both the physical movements *and* the thought they express. An action may thus crudely be compared to a parcel, of which the wrappings represent the external behaviour, and the contents represent the internal thinking. We can only be said fully to understand an action when we know both what it looked like to external observers and what was going on in the mind of the agent. And when our action is defined in this way, it makes nonsense to speak of 'inferring' the motive from the action; for part of what we mean by the action is the motive. What really happens when an historian is said to 'understand' an action is that he

---

[1] See Collingwood, *Idea of History*, p. 301: 'Yet if I not only read his argument but understand it . . . the process of argument which I go through is not a process resembling Plato's, it actually is Plato's . . .'

is aware of two, inseparably connected, goings-on—the physical movements and the thoughts they express. But he is aware of these two processes in different ways: so far as the physical movements are concerned, he is aware of them either by his own eyesight or by reading descriptions and reports of other observers who were aware of them by their eyesight; so far as the motives, intentions, &c. are concerned, he is aware of them by 'rethinking them within his own mind', by 'recreating the experience of the agent .

It may be objected to this account that it contradicts the premises from which it started, since it was originally stated that the motives were the *causes* of a person's actions. Yet we have now reached a position where it would seem improper to speak of 'causes' at all. 'Motives' are 'insides' in some sense, and it is difficult to see how a cause could ever be termed the 'inside' of the event which constitutes its effect. Nevertheless, it is perhaps partially in this very fact that the attraction of the theory we have been discussing resides. It compromises, on the one hand, between the various reasons which incline us to say that motives are not like causes (for example, we feel that to know what somebody's motive was for performing an action is to understand it in a peculiarly *satisfying* way, and to say that such-and-such an action was the *expression* of such-and-such a motive is natural while it seems very much less natural to say that such-and-such an effect was the expression of such-and-such a cause), and, on the other, with the various reasons which incline us to say that motives *are* like causes, namely, those features of our talk about motives alluded to already. Moreover, it eliminates the suggestion that we must always *infer* the motives or grounds of another person's actions, when it frequently appears to be the case that we say or know why somebody did something spontaneously or 'intuitively', without the help of any inferential process whatsoever. Finally, it appears to be in accordance with the experience of the historian: historians attach much importance to the imaginative character of their work, to the need for entering into sympathetic understanding with a personality or a period,

and for 'getting inside' the characters who absorb their
interest.

The main tenets of this theory may be summarized as
follows:

1. Many of the explanations that are given of human conduct are explanations containing reference to intentions,
   resolutions, desires, hopes, plans, calculations, and so
   forth.
2. History, since it is the study of what people have done
   in the past, is necessarily intimately concerned with
   giving explanations of this kind.
3. The intentions, thoughts, and so on to which these
   explanations refer are causes of human actions. They are
   peculiar causes, however, (a) because they are not observable in the ordinary sense, (b) because they form an
   integral part of the physical actions they are said to
   'explain', (c) because we come to know them, not by
   inference in accordance with past experience, but by a
   process of reliving them or re-experiencing them within
   our own minds.

Now if this view is right, it is clear that it brings a number
of new problems in its wake. There are the questions, discussed in Part II, § 4, concerning the status of these mysterious
occult causes operating behind the scenes. There is the question of the relationship of this realm of causes with the realm
of observable physical causes which, as we have seen, is also
referred to by historians in their explanations: the predica-
ment of the human being becomes similar to that of a frail
craft, hurried along on the one hand by the tides of physical
determinism—he does the things he does because of his
environment, his education, his heredity, his nervous system,
the organization of his brain-cells—and, on the other hand,
battered by the gales of a mental or psychical causation—his
intentions, his impulses, his calculations. Between these two
sets of 'forces' the human being, by now a shadowy and in-
determinate ghost, neither truly mental nor truly physical,

precariously subsists, leaving it to the philosophers of the rival 'materialist' and 'idealist' factions to debate endlessly which are the ultimate directors of his destiny. Thirdly, there is the question of the nature of the extra means of knowing that has been postulated as a necessary part of the historian's equipment. Finally, there is the general obscurity, far from being clarified by the metaphorical language wherein it has been stated, that attaches to the relationship between the 'inside' and the 'outside' of the action and to the sense in which the former may be said to 'explain' the latter, when the avenue of ordinary causal explanation has been blocked.

§ 3. *Motives, Other Minds, and 'Understanding'*

In assessing the above answer to the problem before us, there are three principal points which must carefully be distinguished. The first concerns the analysis of the types of explanation we have been considering, the second concerns the nature of our knowledge of what is happening in the minds of other people, and the third concerns the question of 'reliving' or 'recreating' the thoughts and experiences of other people. These three points have frequently been confused, but should be kept separate. We shall examine them in turn.

    1. What does it mean to give an explanation of somebody's action in terms of what he wants, intends, or plans?

Ordinary language, for reasons both of economy and force, is packed with elliptical and metaphorical expressions. This is particularly true of expressions that are said to describe the 'workings of the mind'. The phrase 'the workings of the mind' itself suggests a machine or engine. And we also speak of people being 'occupied by certain thoughts', 'guided by certain considerations', 'governed by certain desires', and 'driven by certain impulses'. We talk of men 'doing what their reason tells them', 'obeying their instincts', 'searching their consciences', and 'fighting their temptations'. And we ask questions like: 'Is he really the victim of delusions of grandeur?' and 'How far are his actions prompted by an overmastering will to power?'

It would be foolish to *criticize* expressions like these, to adopt towards them a tone of puritanical disapproval. From the point of view of ordinary communication they serve their purpose in a convenient and often vivid way. It is not the task of the philosopher to alter people's linguistic habits or whittle away the richness and variety of everyday speech. But it is at least a very important part of his task to prevent the occurrence of philosophical confusions; and this can often be achieved by underlining metaphors when they occur and by pointing to the logical limits of figurative expressions.

These limits may be brought out in the present instance by considering one or two examples. An historian tells us that Napoleon's actions were motivated by a will to power. What was this 'will to power'? Was it like the force that drives a locomotive, a spiritual steam which made its appearance whenever he took a decision or drafted an order? Could its manifestations be observed, timed, predicted, reported upon? Did Napoleon feel them coming on? Did they stop before he lifted his pen or opened his mouth, or was he aware of them persisting simultaneously with his actions? Were they always present, whether he was engaged in activity or not, like a toothache? What happened when he was asleep? Could his urge to power be turned off when he grew tired of it?

Questions like these are useful in making clear the boundaries within which it is safe to use the expression 'he was motivated by a will to power'. For example, when an historian uses it about Napoleon, his usage is considered in this case to be correct if he is able to give instances of Napoleon seizing opportunities that led to an increase in his prestige and authority, rejecting other courses of action which would have led to different results, working hard upon plans and projects for his personal advancement, showing irritation when he was frustrated, reporting perhaps in a diary, or in letters, or in memoirs, upon his aims, his feelings, or his moods. To seek to discover whether Napoleon was in fact motivated by a will to power (as opposed, for example, to being motivated by a desire to inflict suffering or to compensate for a frustrated creative 'drive') is in fact to ask questions of a very different kind from the kind of questions we should ask if we wished to determine whether an engine was driven by steam (as opposed to oil or electricity). For to ask how Napoleon's mind worked is not like asking how a locomotive works.

As a second example, take the sentence 'Richelieu's policy was guided throughout by his aim to establish a centralized French monarchy'. Once again there is a temptation to substantialize the aim, to assimilate it to cases of physical transactions and suppose that an aim guides a man in the same way as rails guide trains, dogs guide men, or friends guide the steps of blind people. Alternatively it may perhaps be regarded as a guide in the same sense as a beacon is a guide, or a lighthouse, signalling to the traveller from the distance, leading him on. But such suppositions are plainly absurd. Or, again, it might appear that there existed 'within Richelieu's mind' some process that continued throughout a particular section of his career called 'the aim of creating a centralized French monarchy', in which case we might be inclined to ask questions concerning the precise length of time this process lasted, the moment at which it 'came on' and the moment at which it finished, whether it manifested itself in short spells or in waves or whether he was always aware of it taking its remorseless course and shadowing him wherever he was and in whatever he did. On the other hand, it might be suggested that Richelieu's aim was something that subsisted in the future and acted upon him by means of a mysterious form of causation in reverse. Yet both of these interpretations would be wrong. The second is a form of nonsense. The first is incorrect: we do not have aims in the way that we have, e.g., toothaches, they do not start and finish, but are *decided upon*, and *realized* or *frustrated*, as the case may be. We cannot speak of 'experiencing an aim' although we can and do speak of 'having an aim'; and, although it may be true that we sometimes experience certain feelings as well, there are not, so far as I am aware, any specific 'aim-sensations'.

If these views are rejected, what is the correct analysis of the sentence 'Richelieu's policy was guided by his aim to establish a centralized French monarchy'? It might still be argued that, even if we discard the belief that some kind of continuous mental process is involved, at any rate a mental act or event *is* involved. If by this it is meant that at some time or other Richelieu formulated a proposition like 'My actions must serve the end of centralizing France' and worked out, either in his head or on paper, a plan by which this could be achieved, there is no great reason to quarrel. When we are speaking of people having aims or intentions it is, I think, as a rule taken for granted that they should be able to put what they are doing and why they are doing it into words. But it appears to me to be far from clear that when we refer to a person's having an aim or an intention we always mean simply and solely that the aim or intention in question was, or even that under certain circumstances it might have been, stated; still less that the pronouncement *caused* all the subsequent actions. We are also interested, when we ask whether a person's aim is such as he tells us or such as has been noted down by him informally in a diary or letter, in the matter of his *keeping to* what he has said he will do, of his putting it into practice. This is as true when we come to assess our own behaviour as when we are assessing that of other people. 'I know I told myself that I would help him, but has that really been my aim?' is not a nonsense question; it is a question for which there exist well-recognized methods of reaching a decision. We do not confine ourselves to judging *others* by their actions. And this is borne out by the fact that when we are referring solely to that which a person thinks, or frankly and openly says, he is going to do, we often introduce qualifications: 'at that precise moment he *really* did *quite honestly* intend . . .'[1]

In contrast to theorists who maintain that words like 'intentions' or 'aims' function as names of causal processes or events

---

[1] It should be added, though, that the mere statement of the intention is not enough in most cases to justify such a claim as this. The *way* in which it was said, its context, and the surrounding circumstances, are all relevant.

pushing from 'within', I want to suggest that to say that a man's actions are guided by such-and-such an intention is to make a statement of varying degrees of complexity about *him* (not about him *plus* the intentions or aims which influence, affect, or 'act upon' him).[1] Such a statement is analysable into both categorical and hypothetical elements in much the same manner as is the case with the statement concerning Napoleon's will to power, although there are significant and obvious differences. The criterion of either having given, or being ready to give, specific reasons for his actions will, for instance, play an extremely important role in the case of statements about a man's intentions, whereas this criterion may play an unimportant role in the case of statements about his desires, 'drives', instincts, and so forth. In general it would be unsafe to ignore the extent to which reference to verbal or symbolic formulation of one kind or another is (or is not) involved in our usage of words like 'intend', 'plan', 'desire', &c. when we are speaking of human beings.[2]

It may now be asked: How, if the account given is correct, are we to interpret *explanations* in terms of motives, desires, intentions, and so forth? For on our theory it cannot be the case that an explanation of the form '*x* did *y* because he wanted *z* (or because his intention was *w*)' refers to the existence of a causal relation between two events. And with this I should agree. But it does not for this reason follow that such statements do not in *any* sense explain. This point may be illuminated by considering as a convenient, if crude, model such a statement as 'John hit you with a hammer because he is bad-tempered'. It would be absurd to deny that this is an

[1] Cf. L. S. Stebbing: '. . . motives are thought to compel *me*. The duality is strangely persistent in our thinking. It is responsible for the wholly unwarrantable separation of the self from *its* acts, of the motive from the act, of the act from the choice, and of the decision from the thing done. . . . We speak of ourself as enslaved to our passions and then as constrained by our motives. We go on to ask what compels the motive . . .' *Philosophy and the Physicists*, p. 181 (Pelican Edition).

[2] A disregard of this point is partly responsible for the inadequacy of Russell's account of desire in *The Analysis of Mind*. Absence of 'quiescence' after eating an apple at t_2 does not necessarily falsify my assertion that I desired to eat an apple at t_1.

explanation: but it would be equally ludicrous to imagine that it could in some manner be 'reduced' to an explanation asserting a causal relation between two events or processes, one of which is labelled 'John's bad temper'. 'John is bad-tempered' is a sentence which, amongst other things, is predictive of how John is likely to behave in various (only vaguely indicated) types of situations. The function of the 'because' in the statement alluded to is to set a statement referring to a specific action within the context of a general statement about John's behaviour which can be 'unpacked' into an indefinite range of statements concerning his reactions to various kinds of circumstances. It represents, if you like, an *instance* of how he can in general be expected to behave under certain conditions. It sets John's action within a pattern, the pattern of his normal behaviour.

It is in terms of this usage of 'explanation', rather than in terms of the cause–effect usage, that historians' (and ordinary persons') accounts of human actions of the kind we are considering are to be understood. This is not to say that it would be correct to bundle together into an amorphous heap historical explanations referring to desires, intentions, purposes, plans, and programmes, as if there were not important differences between them. To say that an individual's actions were planned or conformed to a programme or policy may be very different from saying that they were intended; and again, to say that they were intended can be different from saying that they were motivated by such-and-such a desire. And these cases again are different from those in which we say that his actions were 'reasoned' or 'considered'. But in all these instances it is with explanation in the sense of fitting a particular action within a certain pattern that we are concerned. The patterns are familiar to us both from experience of our own behaviour and from experience of the ways other people behave; and it is in virtue of this that we are able to make the inferences and provide the explanations in question.

2. What does it mean to say that we know what is happening, or what did happen, in the mind of another person?

To deal at length with the philosophical problem of 'other minds' would be to go far beyond the limits of the present work. Nevertheless, since some of the difficulties attached to it have influenced discussions of historical explanation, one or two aspects of the problem may be treated as relevant here.

A common theory of the mind is that which depicts it as a locked chamber to which only one person has direct access— the 'owner'. It is hence concluded that, since the mind is the repository of all a person's emotions, thoughts, and motives, only the owner can truly be said to *know* what his emotions, thoughts, or motives were upon a particular occasion. As a 'privileged observer', he stands unique; to others it is all a matter of suppositions, guesses, and shots in the dark.

The restriction upon the word 'knowledge' here is, however, a peculiar one. For it is not a case of our not being able to know what we could know, given the presence of certain very favourable and unfortunately unattainable conditions; the point is that in the sense of 'know' being offered, it would be self-contradictory to say that another person knew my feelings, my intentions, or my thoughts.

How has this view affected theories of historical explanation? To begin with, if it is true that historians discuss the thoughts and intentions of historical characters, it seems odd to say that they can never really know what these thoughts and intentions were. It may be argued that what they say about them are only hypotheses or conjectures; but it has not been so frequently recognized that this too implies a strange state of affairs. For in our ordinary use of terms like 'conjecture' or 'hypothesis' we suggest that we are resigning ourselves to what is only second-best, a substitute for the real thing. 'I think there may be a man in that cupboard' is a conjecture only: but it implies that we know what it would be like to be *absolutely certain* that a man is concealed in the cupboard. But if all the statements historians (and ordinary people) make about what is happening in the minds of other persons are *necessarily* conjectures, the expression 'to *know* what someone else is thinking' has no use in our language. It is excluded by the restriction placed upon the word 'know'. And in consequence words like 'conjecture' or 'hypothesis' may no longer be contrasted with 'knowledge' as it occurs in this kind of context.

The above rigid limitation has had its consequences for the philosophy of history. For it leads to an attempt to remove what appears to be an intolerable doubt regarding the validity of historical knowledge. This doubt has been dealt with, as we have seen, by the expedient of saying that the historian literally 'relives' the experiences, thoughts, and so forth of the historical agents with whom he is concerned, that he has the *same* thoughts, the *same* motives which they had, and hence can truly be said to know what these were. Of this there is more to be said below. Here, however, we must ask whether the original doubt which the theory mentioned is alleged to resolve is, in fact, a genuine one.

I think it is not, for the following reason. The picture of people 'owning' minds of whose contents they are 'privileged observers' is a misleading one. For it immediately suggests an analogy between emotions, sensations, thoughts, on the one hand, and physical objects on the other. (Hence expressions like 'motives are causes seen from the inside'. Consider also the phrase 'mental furniture'.) And from this it seems to follow that it is an empirical obstacle that prevents us from knowing what goes on in someone else's mind. But this misses the point. Knowledge of other minds is not causally but *logically* impossible if we restrict knowledge of feeling or thinking something to the person who actually has the feeling or the thought. And this is because 'having a feeling' is not like 'having an edition of Proust'. It is not something which can be produced for another person to inspect. Even telepathic communication would not do the trick: for here again it is *I* who am having the feeling, which I judge to be correlated with yours. I am not, in the strict sense required, having *your* feeling.

What is not recognized by those who are haunted by this

metaphysical doubt is that there is a use for the expression 'I know what he is feeling (or thinking)', and that this expression may meaningfully be contrasted with the expression 'I think he is feeling so-and-so, but of course I am only guessing', or 'I imagine this is what he is feeling'. And this use of 'knowing what another person is feeling' has nothing to do with *being* the person in question. I may, for example, be said to *know* that another person is feeling pain if he tells me so in certain circumstances which would preclude the possibility of his lying. I may be said to *know* what another person's motives are if he tells me, openly and easily, that they are such-and-such. The conditions under which it is correct to say we 'know' vary: the important point is that the verification of an hypothesis concerning what is happening in someone else's mind consists in obtaining this *kind* of information; it does not consist in 'having his experience',[1] for, as we have seen, we can give no meaning to this phrase.

    3. What meaning can be attached to such expressions as 'reliving the experiences of other people', 'rethinking the thoughts of historical characters', and the like?

An argument that has often been brought forward in support of the view that the procedure of the historian is *sui generis* is the assertion that historians often speak of 'living themselves into' the minds of the people whose actions they wish to explain. We also hear of 'historical insight' and 'intuitive understanding'.

This suggests that historians are in possession of an additional power of knowing which allows them to 'penetrate into' the minds of the subjects of their study and take, as it were, psychological X-ray photographs. We have seen why the postulation of such a power has seemed necessary to some philosophers; we have now to try to discover what precisely is meant by mention of 'insight' and 'reliving past thoughts' and whether this entails the existence of any such additional power.

---

[1] 'Having the same experience' in the sense of 'having a similar experience' is, of course, another matter.

Let us consider two occasions on which phrases of this sort might be used:

(*a*) An historian or a detective, when asked to explain how he reached a particular conclusion regarding the motives or reasons for a person's actions, might say: 'I put myself into his position, and imagined why I should have done that kind of thing in those circumstances, i.e. what my intention or plan would have been, what reasons I should have had' (not 'what would have *caused* me to do it'). To express this more concisely the historian or detective *might* (at a pinch) say 'I re-thought myself into his mind', or, even less plausibly, 'I revived within myself his thoughts'. But he would not thereby be describing some strange process with the aid of which he *became* the person whose actions he was trying to explain, or established direct contact with his inner life. The question he originally asked himself was: 'What was X trying to achieve by performing that set of actions?' The way he answered it was by imagining what he himself would have been trying to achieve if he had carried out the same actions. In this manner, he used his own experience of what it is to do something for certain reasons or purposes as a *guide* to discovering X's reasons or purposes. And there is surely nothing particularly mysterious about such a procedure. Nor is he formulating anything more than an hypothesis. He may be wrong. And the way in which he decides whether he is right or wrong does not consist of getting still closer to X's thoughts in some peculiar way: it consists in seeing how far other facts, facts about X's past history, later behaviour, words spoken under cross-examination, and so forth, tally with such an interpretation. It has too often been the case that philosophers of history have identified a useful method for arriving at hypotheses concerning the motives for human action with the confirmation of the hypotheses thus arrived at.[1] 'When in doubt as to why a person did something, put yourself in his position' may be

---

[1] See Max Weber, *The Theory of Social and Economic Organisation*, p. 88: 'More generally, verification of subjective interpretation by comparison with the concrete course of events is, as in the case of all hypotheses, indispensable.'

a useful methodological precept, but it is far from always being reliable. People differ. From the fact that, if I did x, it would be because I wanted y, i.e. would have been satisfied if y occurred, would have given y as my aim if asked, &c., it does not follow that when a medieval baron did x he wanted y. To find out whether y was really the reason for someone's doing x, we need more facts, not more intuition.

(*b*) We often hear of historians 'understanding' the actions of historical agents. And it is pointed out that 'understanding an action' is different from 'understanding an event'. This distinction is important but it is easy to misinterpret it.

Let us suppose that someone of our acquaintance is behaving very oddly towards us: let us further suppose that it suddenly comes to our knowledge that this person has been informed that we have done or said something which has annoyed him. We may say: 'Now I can *understand* why he is being so peculiar.' When we use the word 'understand' in such a context what we say has reference to our knowledge of how we should feel and behave if we found ourselves in a similar situation. And this is a different use of the word from that which it has in such a case as the following: it is explained to me for the first time that winter in England is colder than summer because of a difference in the position of England with regard to the sun's rays, and I say: 'Now I understand.' For, in the latter case, my 'understanding' is connected with my seeing the relation between a particular natural occurrence and a general law about the transmission of heat from the sun. Or take a statement like this: 'The watching of public executions was common amongst people of Pepys' time, and I suppose that explains why he used to go to them. But nowadays it is rather difficult for us to understand it.' And what this means is that we cannot imagine ourselves enjoying a public execution. The rider, 'I can't see myself doing it', is present. Nor is our usage of the word 'understand' confined to cases where the emotions of other people are concerned. We can also be said to understand their actions, when it is a case of their acting skilfully, prudently, decorously, cautiously, and so forth. We appreciate the performance of certain actions by other people when we ourselves have had experience of what it is to do those same actions, when we also know *how*.[1]

Some philosophers might be tempted to interpret the fact that we are often able to 'perform this feat of understanding' as an indication that we are able to make direct contact with other people's thoughts and feelings. For they might argue that it seems to be psychologically false that our understanding in such cases is the result of an analogical argument of the type illustrated in (*a*) above. Understanding of the kind we have described is an immediate unreflective process, which does not consist of an elaborate prior ratiocination based upon the 'assumption' that other people feel, think, and behave much as we ourselves do. And this, of course, is true. But it does not follow therefrom that when we are said to understand someone's feelings or motives, or appreciate his skill or intelligence, we are intuiting mysterious agencies 'behind the scenes', any more than when we say 'I see what you mean' we imply that there is something in our field of vision called a 'meaning'. What understanding, in this sense, does presuppose is that he who understands should have had experience of what it is to feel or do certain things. Compare the cases of the man who can drive and the man who cannot drive when they sit in a car driven by another person. And consider the kind of reply that is often made to the remark: 'I cannot conceive why he should have behaved like that.' We say: 'You wouldn't be able to—you are not that sort of person', or 'You have never been engaged in doing the sort of thing he was doing'.

It may be objected that very often, in the case of the historian, for example, understanding is assessed in terms of a capacity to account for action by extraordinary persons in unfamiliar situations. And this is also true of the insight into character which we ascribe to certain novelists and poets—Dostoievsky's creation of Raskolnikov, for instance, Proust's creation of Charlus, Shakespeare's heroes. And what happens

---

[1] See G. Ryle, *The Concept of Mind*, chap. ii.

when we read the case-books of neurotic behaviour provided by a psychologist? Why do we so often feel that the analyses given are 'right', although the behaviour and emotions recorded are frequently of a kind remote from our own experience?

'Imaginative understanding', as we might call it, seems to involve a capacity on the part of some people to go beyond their own limited experience of what it is to feel certain emotions and do certain things. But once again it would be misleading to interpret such understanding as equivalent to *becoming* the person whose actions are thus being interpreted. For we can *argue* about such interpretations: we can say they are convincing, plausible, far-fetched, absurd. And the form that such arguments take is revealing. For they rely upon reference either to our own experience or to the reported experience of other people. Extraordinary behaviour by another person may be intelligible to a normal person provided that it bears some likeness—even if this is remote—to what he himself on occasions has done. Is the watching of executions or gladiatorial combats wholly unintelligible to one who enjoys sadistic American films and 'tough' novels? It is significant that the first of Freud's 'Introductory Lectures' dealt with the kind of errors, slips, and so forth ordinary people make in their ordinary day-to-day affairs, and the second with the·common occurrence of dreams. An important part of imagination or insight consists, I suggest, in the ability to recognize resemblances between apparently very different experiences.

In what has been said, I have not wished to disparage the part played in historical writing by 'insight', 'intuition', and what is signified by related terms.[1] Such terms are not meaningless when used in ordinary discourse, but they are open to abuse. The word 'intuition', for example, is particularly open to this because there is a technical usage of the term—when,

---

[1] For an excellent presentation of a view that emphasizes the intuitive element in the writing of history, see Prof. H. A. Hodges, *Wilhelm Dilthey: an Introduction*. Dilthey's understanding of how historians do in fact work was often profound and illuminating: it is the epistemological conclusions that he drew which seem to me to be invalid.

for example, philosophers speak of 'intuiting universals', 'intuiting essences', and so on—with which it is easily confused. When 'intuition' is used to describe the kind of imaginative understanding which we have been considering, on the other hand, difficulties of a metaphysical nature do not arise. It is instead seen to be a *way* by which we interpret other people's behaviour: it is not knowledge of another order achieved by an identification of our thoughts, feelings, &c., with theirs or by an abstruse technique for looking into their minds. Belief in the existence of such knowledge has its roots in the systematic ambiguity of expressions like 'having the same thought', 'reaching the same conclusion', and 'acting with the same motive'.

§ 4. *Re-examination of the Problem*

How do the considerations of the previous section affect the problem with which we are concerned?

This, it will be remembered, involved those explanations historians provide that are given in terms of human motives, purposes, plans, and the like. The problem was a twofold one. It was asked: (1) What is the correct analysis of those explanations? and (2) what justifies an historian's providing such explanations? And it was seen that philosophers have suggested that, although motives and intentions *cause* human actions, they are causes of a peculiar kind, which can only strictly be said to be known by the agent himself. Hence arose the view that they are hidden entities, lying within human actions as the kernel lies within a nut, and that, since we cannot observe them when we are examining the activities of other people, we must in some sense re-experience them or relive them within our own minds.

Like so many philosophical theories, this one has developed out of the recognition of a genuine distinction; but the distinction has been misinterpreted and the solution suggested raises, as was pointed out, a host of additional problems. And it has been argued that, instead of regarding motivational explanations as referring to causes of a peculiar kind, we should recognize that they are not causal at all. In this manner, we obviate the difficulty that arises as soon as we imagine that the motives of other people are things or processes which we can only come to know of in some manner analogous to (although not the same as) the manner we come to know what caused the lights to go out, namely, by an inspection of the fuse-box.

As against this, it has been argued that to speak of a person having a motive, aim, or plan is to make a shorthand, and often rather indefinite, statement about him. It is not to talk about him and, in addition, something else which makes him act as he does. To suppose that this is the case is to make a mistake analogous to, although not the same as, the mistake philosophers have made who have postulated the existence of an underlying 'substance' to account for the sensible appearances of things.

What makes the picture of motives as invisible causes so attractive is the fact that people, before doing something, often work out 'in their heads' how they are going to achieve a certain result. About this the following observations may be made. (1) *Part* of what we mean when we say that an action is 'intentional' or 'done for a purpose' may be that at some time or another a certain plan has been formulated by the agent to which the action *conforms*. (2) When we decide, *in our own case*, why we did something on a particular occasion we do not perform a mysterious act of 'looking inside' for mental entities called 'motives'—we may, on the other hand, do it by remembering how we formulated the matter to ourselves before we acted, but we may also do it by recalling the kind of reasons we should have given if someone had asked us what we were about either during or after the performance of the action in question; and we may again do it in some cases by ignoring the ostensible reasons we gave to ourselves or to others and by considering instead other factors such as our reactions and feelings when a certain state of affairs was brought about, the kind of context in which the action was performed (perhaps its similarities with other occasions upon which we have acted in the past), and our knowledge of our own character and personality. (3) When we are called upon to decide why a person other than ourselves acted as he did, the criteria we use are always and necessarily what he does or what he tells us. The inference involved when we infer that someone else has such-and-such an aim or motive is inference to what on actual occasions he has done or said or to what on hypothetical occasions he would do or say. The demand that the criteria should be the same both in cases where we are deciding upon the nature of our own motives and in cases where we are deciding upon the nature of the motives of another person is an illegitimate one, and its origin must be attributed to the assimilation of talk about motives and actions to talk about causes and effects.

It may be objected that we make use of our own experience when we are assessing the motives of others. This must be, and has been, admitted. But to admit it is not to admit the proposition frequently alleged to follow from it, that our own experience is in some way transformed into the experience of the person whose motives we are examining, that when, for example, an historian is said to understand why Caesar crossed the Rubicon he becomes Caesar and intuitively rethinks in his own mind thoughts which are literally identical with Caesar's thoughts on the occasion in question. We all know (it would be an abuse of language to say that we 'assume') that people often act rationally, that in many situations they can be counted upon to give us good reasons for that which they are doing and to do it in a certain kind of way. As rational beings ourselves, accustomed to choose between various methods of attaining certain results, it is not surprising that we are able, readily and often without hesitation, to understand why, in similar situations, other people have acted as they have, and to imagine the sort of reasons they would have given for the actions they performed, had they been asked. That it should have been thought that there is a mystery about this is itself a mystery.

Again, it might be objected that, in the case of historical

personalities, who are dead, buried, and eternally mute, we can never be said on our theory truly to 'know' what they were about. And once again the bogy of the unverifiable motive-hypothesis is raised to scare us into the admission that there is something 'funny' about historical knowledge. But what more is required? What kind of evidence would satisfy our objector? Confessions, memoirs, diaries mislaid and discovered years later—all would be irrelevant. For the diarist, the author of memoirs, might be cheating, deliberately writing for posterity: worse still, he might be 'deceiving himself'. And how should we set about deciding whether he was doing these things or not? Once more, by using the kind of tests we do use in such cases; by examining what we know of his other behaviour, of the time at which he lived, of the situation in which he was placed, perhaps by comparing what.he did with what we should have done in like circumstances.[1] These represent the kind of criteria historians are in the habit of applying. More they cannot do. And the impossibility involved is not a causal or physical impossibility—there is no empirical barrier—but, as has been said, a logical one. The only state of affairs which would satisfy our objector would be one in which the historian actually *was* all the characters about whom he writes.

We should by now be clear that the conflict supposed to exist between materialistic and idealistic interpretations of history is an illusory one. We are not confronted by two realms of causes intersecting or running across one another. What we are confronted by are various uses of the word 'explain'. To explain a person's action by giving the purpose it is designed to serve is not the same as to explain an action by referring to

---

[1] 'The real reasons' (e.g. for an action) is an expression almost as open to abuse as the expression 'the real causes'. Indeed, the two phrases are frequently referred to as if they were identical in meaning, a fact responsible for considerable confusion. In general, it appears safe to say that by a man's 'real reasons' we mean those reasons he would be prepared to give under circumstances where his confession would not entail adverse consequences to himself. An exception to this is the psycho-analyst's usage of the expression where different criteria are adopted.

a physical event or situation which caused it. And explanations in terms of reasons given, plans or policies adopted, principles followed, are likewise distinct from causal explanations. In the final part of this book I have only had space to suggest the lines along which I believe the analysis of explanations involving reference to how people behave and how they do things should proceed; I have not been able to consider such explanations in all the variety of their occurrence in history books. But what I have been concerned to show is the kind of confusions which arise when it is imagined that different types of explanation imply the existence of different types of causes. This is not, of course, to say that it is not possible to give a causal explanation of why it is that a person wants, intends, plans, or calculates something; such explanations, on the contrary, are frequently made. We can say that a boy wants to pass his examination because he has been promised a reward if he does so, that a statesman's actions conform to a certain plan because of information he has received from his ambassador: and we can give explanations of a person's desires in physiological terms—nervous or cerebral processes, for instance, or the behaviour of the ductless glands—as well as in terms of environmental factors acting upon him. Such explanations are as important to the historian as to anyone else. All I have wished to stress is that to speak of a person's having, for example, a desire is not at all the same thing as to speak of his having a carbuncle on his toe or of his suffering from a disturbance of the nervous system, and that the interpretation of explanations containing the former kind of reference must make allowance for this distinction.

Historical materialists and historical idealists have often appeared to stand on opposite sides, one side claiming to give to history a truly scientific status, the other claiming to defend the freedom of the human spirit. On the one hand we find Marx writing:

Upon the different forms of property, upon the social conditions of existence, rises an entire superstructure of distinct and characteristically formed sentiments, illusions, modes of thought and views of life. The entire class creates and forms them out of its material foundations and out of the corresponding social relations.[1]

On the other we find, for instance, Collingwood writing:

> The disappearance of historical naturalism, however, entails the further conclusion that the activity by which man builds his own constantly changing world is a free activity. There are no forces other than this activity which control it or modify it or compel it to behave in this way or in that, to build one kind of world rather than another.[2]

The first quotation suggests that people's thoughts and ideas are a kind of vapour (notice, incidentally, Marx's use of the pejorative terms 'sentiments' and 'illusions') which mysteriously rises from the 'material foundations': but in the second quotation this vapour has been given force and life; it 'controls and modifies' the world, 'compels it to behave in this way or that'. Collingwood admittedly speaks of 'human activity', but it is clear, I think, from what he says subsequently in the section in question that by this activity he means the activity of reason—thoughts, intentions, and plans.

The apparent antinomy created arises out of the view that the world is made up, on the one hand, of 'dead matter', and, on the other, of 'mind'; in human beings it is thought that these are miraculously intermixed. A human being is 'matter' with 'mind' attached. Some philosophers have wanted to emphasize the importance of the former at the expense of the latter, some philosophers have wished to do the opposite. But must we do either? May we not recognize that, although when we speak of human beings having minds we are saying something important and true about them, we are not saying something both about them and about some other entities as well—intentions, wishes, skills, and so on—which operate upon them from without—or, rather, from within? Whether we regard human beings in their 'physical' aspects or in their 'mental' aspects depends upon our interests. The physiologist is interested in the behaviour of the blood-stream, the arrange-

---

[1] *The Eighteenth Brumaire of Louis Bonaparte*, section iii.
[2] *Idea of History*, p. 315.

ment of the brain cells: the psychologist or the historian is interested in what people think, say, feel, do. There is no conflict, only a difference of point of view and purpose. Human beings are not 'really matter' or 'really mind': they are human beings. Different ways of talking about them, dictated by different interests, have been hypostatized into different ingredients.

This confusion has been reflected in monistic theories of historical explanation. We do explain human actions in terms of reaction to environment. But we also explain human actions in terms of thoughts, desires, and plans. We may believe that it is in principle possible to give a full causal explanation of why people think, desire, or plan the things they do in terms of their past experience or training, or perhaps in terms of the workings of their bodies. But, even if the latter proposition is true, it still does not follow that explanation in terms of thoughts and desires has been rendered superfluous, or that it has been 'reduced' to cause–effect explanation. Nor does it follow that human action is never 'free' or 'rational'. The rules for the use of these words are not governed by considerations regarding the possibility of giving a causal explanation.

INDEX